ROLL

of

NEW HAMPSHIRE MEN

at

LOUISBURG, CAPE BRETON

1745

ORIGINALLY PUBLISHED
CONCORD, NEW HAMPSHIRE:
EDWARD N. PEARSON, PUBLIC PRINTER
1896

HERITAGE BOOKS
2018

HERITAGE BOOKS

AN IMPRINT OF HERITAGE BOOKS, INC.

Books, CDs, and more—Worldwide

For our listing of thousands of titles see our website
at
www.HeritageBooks.com

A Facsimile Reprint
Published 2018 by
HERITAGE BOOKS, INC.
Publishing Division
5810 Ruatan Street
Berwyn Heights, Md. 20740

Originally published
Concord, New Hampshire
Edward N. Pearson, Public Printer
1896

International Standard Book Numbers
Paperbound: 978-0-7884-3039-8
Clothbound: 978-0-7884-8896-2

JOINT RESOLUTION TO AUTHORIZE THE GOVERNOR AND
COUNCIL TO APPOINT A PERSON OR PERSONS TO
REPRESENT THE STATE OF NEW HAMPSHIRE AT THE
PROPOSED CELEBRATION AT LOUISBURG.

[$500 appropriated.]

*Resolved by the Senate and House of Representatives in
General Court convened:*

That the governor and council are hereby authorized to
appoint a person or persons to represent the state of New
Hampshire at the proposed celebration of the one hundred
and fiftieth anniversary of the capture of Louisburg, to be
held at Louisburg June 17, 1895. Such representative or
representatives shall receive their actual expenses only, and
the same shall be paid from any money in the treasury not
otherwise appropriated, upon approval of the governor and
council. The governor and council are hereby further
authorized to cause to be printed not exceeding two thousand copies of the report of such representative or representatives, together with the names of the soldiers from
New Hampshire who served at the capture of Louisburg,
and all of the historical facts connected therewith, the same
to be distributed as follows: One copy to each representative and senator of the New Hampshire legislature, one copy
to each state officer, one copy to each Grand Army post in
the state, one copy to each town library in the state, and
the balance to be deposited in the state library and disposed
of by the trustees thereof in the same manner as other
publications deposited therein. The total expenditure
under this resolution shall not exceed five hundred dollars.

[Approved March 28, 1895.]

Session Laws of 1895, chapter 138.

His Excellency
CHARLES A. BUSIEL, Governor,
And the Honorable Council,

Appointed the writer special commissioner to represent New Hampshire at the proposed celebration at Louisburg, Cape Breton, June 17, 1895, collect the historical facts, names of the New Hampshire soldiers and sailors in the expedition, and cause the same to be published.

After one hundred and fifty years have come and gone since the events took place, with the loss of all the muster rolls and many other documents that would throw light on the subject, I find the best explanation of the situation by Hon. Charles Hudson of Lexington, Mass., in the New England Genealogical and Antiquarian Register, Vol. 24, 367 : " Every antiquary who has attempted to explore that field must have been disappointed in not being able to find a list of the gallant men who served in the memorable expedition to Cape Breton in 1745, when the undisciplined militia of New England took Louisburg from the veteran troops of France. It will be recollected that that expedition originated with the colony, and was executed by colonial troops. The bravery displayed and the complete success which crowned the enterprise attracted attention across the Atlantic, so that the mother country readily assumed the act and paid the cost of the expedition. To adjust these accounts it became necessary that they should have the rolls, and they were accordingly sent to England, and have never been returned. In fact, the same is true of the records of the council of that day ; they were sent to the home government, and the copies now in the archives of the state are transcripts from the original records. No such copies of these rolls have ever been made, and hence our archives furnish no lists of these brave men. Feeling the great need of some such list, I have endeavored to collect from all sources within my reach, the names of the officers and soldiers who served in that campaign. But I have found the task more difficult than I anticipated. In the first place, but few of the lists I have been able to find give the residence of the officers or soldiers, so that in many cases it is difficult to determine even to what state certain men or detachments belong. Neither do the lists I have been able to find profess to be full or perfect. In fact they are not properly rolls of the companies. They are, rather, partial reports of the sanitary condition of certain detachments at particular stations, or of the men assigned to a particular command, or the signers of petitions for a certain object, or the names of those who empowered a certain person to act as their agent in receiving their bounty or share of the spoils. In some cases we have only the notice that such an one is in the hospital, or is dead, or is discharged for inability. I have thought it due to the public to make this statement, that they may see how much dependence may be placed upon the lists I propose to give. I cannot say that they are perfect, or entirely reliable, but only that I have used my best endeavors to make them as perfect as my means would allow, and I flatter myself that my labors have not been entirely in vain."

This description of the situation of affairs by Mr. Hudson applies as well to New Hampshire as to Massachusetts. The number of men from New Hampshire in the expedition when it sailed for Louisburg was 502. Recruits, 120 at least, and probably more. Have found the names of 496 men, leaving 126 unaccounted for. The residences of the men, as given, are the writer's.

The writer is under great obligations to Senator Gallinger, who called the attention of Secretary Olney to the missing muster-rolls and, through him, of Minister Bayard in England, where the rolls undoubtedly went as vouchers, although no clue to them has been obtained there yet.

We hope our members of congress, with the assistance

of the delegations from Massachusetts, Rhode Island, and Connecticut, will secure an appropriation from the government to enable further investigations to be made, and, if possible, to obtain copies of the rolls, in order that justice may be done to the memory of the brave men who captured Louisburg.

GEORGE C. GILMORE,

Special Commissioner.

Manchester, N. H., Sept. 25, 1896.

The provincial government of New Hampshire in 1745 consisted of a royal governor, council, and assembly.

Governor.

BENNING WENTWORTH.

Council.

George Jaffrey,
Jotham Odiorn,
Henry Sherburne,
Joseph Sherburne,
Ellis Huske,
Theodore Atkinson,
Samuel Solley,
John Downing,
Richard Wibird,
Samuel Smith.

Assembly.

Province of ⎰ Anno Regni Regis Georgii Secundi, Magnæ
New Hamp^r ⎱ Brittaniæ, Franciæ et Hiberniæ, Decimo Octavo, &c.

A Journal of the House of Representatives at a General Assembly of his Majesty's Province of New Hampshire in

New Engl^d began and held at Portsm° in s^d Province on Thursday 24 January, Anno Dom: 1745.

Portsm°	Nathaniel Rogers, Esq Eleazer Russell, Esq Henry Sherburn, jun.
Dover	Coll. Thomas Wallingford Thomas Millet, Esq. Capt. John Winget
Hampton Hampton Falls	Sam¹ Palmer, Esq. Mr. Joseph Philbrook Mr. Meshech Wear
Exeter	Col. Peter Gilman Mr. Zeb. Gideons
Stretham	Moses Levitt, Esq.
New Castle	William Frost, Esq.
Rye	Jonathan Lock
Kingston	Maj^r Eben^r Stevens, Esq.
Greenland	Clement March, Esq.
*Newington	George Walton, Esq.
New Market	Capt. Israel Gilman
Durham	Capt Jonathan Thompson
Londonderry	Mr John Wallace, Sen

Friday Feby 1. Declared by the House, not legally elected, and dismissed.

Feby 12. Mr. Secretary, Coll. Downing & Mr. Wibird came into the House & declaring they were sent to qualify John Fabyan, Esq. adminis^d the oath to him, & he took his place in ye House being directed thereto by the speaker.

Journal of the House.

Fryday, Feby 1st 1745. Met according to adjournm^t & all ye members present.

Richd Wibird Esq. brought down a letter from his Exc^y Govr Shirley with some papers Relating to the proceedings of the Gov^t of the Mass. Bay on an intended Expedition to Louisburg.

* Elected to fill the vacancy caused by the dismissal of George Walton, Esq.

Governor Shirley's Communication.

Province of the   }
Massachusetts Bay }

The Committee of both Houses upon the subject of his Excellency's messages of the 19th & 22[d] instant make the following report, viz.

That they have been attended by two Gentlemen who have lately been prisoners at Louisburg & by others who have been traders there & who are well acquainted with the place, from whom the Committee have received information that the Garrison there does not consist of more than five or six hundred regular Troops & that there are not above three or four hundred fighting men of the Inhabitants, that they have but a small stock of Provisions, that they have no vessels of Force in their Harbour, and that the place is at this time less capable of being defended against an attack than its probable, it will be hereafter.

The Committee therefore are of opinion that it is incumbent upon this Government to embrace this favourable opportunity to attempt the reduction thereof; and they humbly propose that his Excell[y] the Capt. General be desired to give forth his Proclamation to encourage the Inlistment of three Thousand Volunteers under such proper officers as he shall appoint, That each person so enlisting be allowed Twenty-five shillings pr month, & that there be delivered to each man a blanket, that one month's pay be advanced & that they be entitled to all the plunder.

That provision be made for the furnishing of necessary warlike stores for the Expedition, That four months provisions be laid in, That a Committee be appointed to procure & fit vessels to serve as Transports to be ready to depart by the beginning of March, and that a suitable naval force be provided for their convoy, as this Court shall hereafter order. That application be forthwith made to the Government of New York, the Jerseys & Pennsylvania, New Hampshire, Connecticutt & Rhode Island to furnish their respective

Quotas of men & vessels to accompany or follow the Forces of this Province.

In the name & by order of the Committee.

Wm. Pepperell.

In Council, Jan. 25, 1745—Read & Sent down.

In the House of Represent[s], Jan, 25, 1745—Read & Accepted. Sent up for concurrence.

T. Cushing, Speak[r].

In Council, Jan. 25, 1745—Read & concurred.

J. Williard, Sec[y].

Consented to

W. Shirley.

Copy examin[d] pr. J. Williard Sec[y].

Saturday, Feb[y] y[e] 2[d] 1745. Met according to adjournment & the Com[te] of both Houses on the subject of Gov[r] Shirleys letter & some other papers laid before the House yesterday by his Exc[y] having made their Report, it was brought into the House by Mr. Downing & Mr. Solly & read as follows:

Province of New Hamp[r].

The Committee of both Houses on the subject of his Excellency Governor Shirleys letter and some other papers laid before the Assembly this day by his Excellency:

The Committee are of opinion that it is incumbent upon this Province to do all they can to forward & encourage the intended Expedition for the Reduction of Louisburg or Cape Breton, and humbly propose that (if proper methods may be concluded on for defraying the charge which the Committee are of opinion will be about four thousand pounds lawfull money) his Excellency the Captain General be desired to give forth his Proclamation to encourage the enlisting of two hundred & fifty volunteers under such proper officers as he shall appoint; that each person so enlisting be allowed Twenty-five shillings pr month & that be delivered to each man a blanket, that one months pay be advanced and that they be entitled to all the plunder; That

provision be made for the furnishing of necessary warlike
stores for the Expedition, that four months provision be
laid in, that a Comittee be appointed to procure & fit ves-
sells to serve as transports to be ready to depart by the
beginning of March.

Feby 1, 1745—   Theodore Atkinson   Peter Gilman
                 Saml Smith   Thos Millet
                 John Downing   Hen. Sherburne
                 Saml Solly.   Moses Leavit.

Voted, That afores^d Report of Com^tee be accepted & sent
up for concurrance.

———

Cape Breton Expedition—Plan of Operations*.

MEM°. In order for the attacking of Louisbourg this
Spring by surprise its propos'd that 3000 Troops should
Embark from hence in Sloops & Schooners and proceed for
Canso, well armed which should be a place of Rendezvous
it being within 20 Leagues of Louisbourg; and its being
uncertain that so many vessels should be able to keep Company together when they are arrived at said Port, to take a
favourable opportunity to sail from thence in order to be at
Gaberous point by Dusk, from whence it is but 3 Leagues
from Louisbourg, then to push into the Bay, and as soon as
said vessels are at an anchor to man as many whaleboats as
they have & send them along the shore as neare as possible,
which will make it the more difficult for them to be discov-
ered, & when they come to the cove which faces the low
part of the wall, there to land if the Sea will permit & scale
that place if possible, & if otherwise as the Wall breaks off
a little on the other side of the East gate, not far from that
there are picketts put for a considerable distance across a
pond over to the Wall on the Beach on the other side of
the Pond, and as this Pond is frozen all the month of March
its not very difficult to get over them : but if the weather

*This paper was laid before the House, with the letter from Governor Shirley.

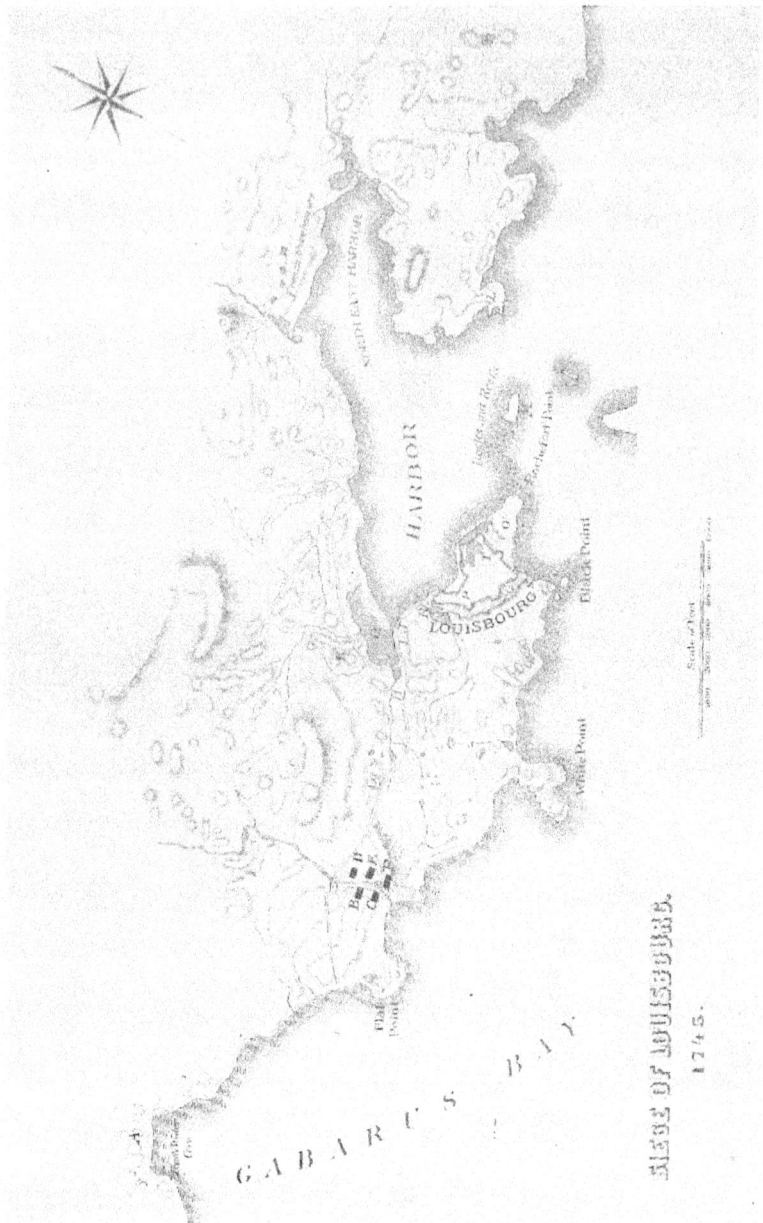

SIEGE OF LOUISBURG.

1745.

Scale of Feet

From "A Half Century of Conflict," by Francis Parkman.

INDEX

TO MAP OF THE SIEGE OF LOUISBOURG, 1745.

A Landing of New England Men.
B Camp of Burr's Regiment.
C   "   " Pepperrell's "
D   "   " Willard's   "
E   "   " Moulton's   "
F   "   " Moore's   "
G First or Green Hill Battery.
H Second Battery.
I Third Battery.
J Fourth, or Advanced Battery.
K Fifth, or Titcomb's Battery.
L Lighthouse Battery.
M Island Battery (French).
N Grand, or Royal Battery (French).
O Burying-ground.
P King's Bastion, or Citadel.
Q Barachois.
R West Gate.
S South Gate.
T Maurepas Gate.

will not permit their landing in the above place let them
proceed along the shore till they come to a long Range of
Rocks that goes towards the Island, at the End of which is
a Passage where the shallops go through, let them go in
there and follow the Ledge of Rocks right back again, then
they will land right against the East gate on a point, and
as there are some Houses there, it will hinder their being
seen, but one Boat ought to go first & surprise the People
in those Houses a little time before the others come up, Each
whale boat must have two ladders in them fifteen foot long
which may be put in the middle of the Boat without hin-
drance to the men ; but the Boatmen must lay still at this
Point till they think the main body is got near the Town,
& that a party of as many men as shall be judg'd proper
shall be ready to attack the Grand Battery, its necessary it
should be low water if no Drift Ice aground along the shore,
for the remainder of the men to go round the Picketts that
are by the north gate, and when they get round with Ladders of 15 feet long, they can scale the Wall facing the
Harbour which is a Quarter of a mile round, and it will be
absolutely necessary to appoint a Time to strike the blow
all at once, which can be done by agreeing upon a certain
hour just before Day, which is the Sleepiest Time, and the
Commanding officer of each Detachment to know the time,
and when the Time comes by his Watch to begin without
further ceremony ; The Enemy finding themselves attacked
at so many different places at once its probable it will breed
such confusion among them that our men will have time to
get in unmolested ; & it is to be observ'd that as the men
march from the above point the low wall is on the left hand
of the gate, and the Picketts on the right hand ; as all the
enemy's troops are in the citadel except a small guard or
two it will be a considerable time before the men are drest
& got ready to march out, and even then it is quite in the
other End of the town.

This is what probably may succeed, but least any accident

should happen to prevent it, it will be necessary to provide accordingly & in case our People should be discover'd & Repuls'd the above number of men being sufficient to command the field, it will be necessary in order to reduce the place to have what shipping can possibly be got to cruise off the Harbour's Mouth in order to intercept their Provision vessels which they Expect early being at this time very short of Provisions, as likewise to take any transports with men if any should come, and that our men may not be discourag'd at being repuls'd once, it will be necessary to send 12 nine pounders & two small mortars with shells, &c. and a Quantity of Provisions, so to bombard them & endeavor to make Breaches in their Walls & then storm them : and should the shipping be so lucky as to take their Provisions and the land forces take all their cattle & keep them constantly employed, it will be impossible for them to hold the place till the last of July for want of provisions.

In order the better to secure the Retreat in case a superiour naval Force to ours should come from France & drive ours off the Coast, it will be necessary to have two small vessels with about Two hundred men at Canso, & the day after the Fleet is sail'd for Louisbourg for them to sail so as to get in by night, and it being but six Leagues from Canso to St. Peters they can get there before day & surprise that place, which is an exceeding good harbour for small vessels, but has not Water sufficient for vessels of that size which will be able to drive ours off the Coast, so that the vessels for the Retreat will lay there safe, and the Troops be able to go to them by Land ; there will be an advantage besides this in surprising this place as there is always a number of Indians with their Families which keep with a French Priest at a small Distance from the French Inhabitants, and the Booty taken there will pay the Expence & more in taking it.   It is to be observed that during the time our Troops lay siege to the Town, it will be in their power to send parties and Destroy all their Fishery on the

Island as well as the north side of the Harbour which would ruin their Fishery for four or five years; and as it is impossible to fail of taking the Royal Battery at least, that would in a great measure lay open their Harbour exposed unto an attack by Sea from England, as the new Batterys in the Town in the greatest part of the Ambrozers, there are no guns & there are two gates that are made in Diamond fashion facing the Harbour that can be beat down in an instant the peices not being but 2 inches & an half thick.

N. B.   The full complement of Troops is 700 out of which deductions must be made of 50 for each of the two Batteries, viz. the Royal & Island Batteries, & 50 for Death, sickness &c. which reduce them to 550, and the other fighting men in the Town do not exceed 300, and that the Swiss Troops which are their best Troops are exceeding Discontented & mutinous; also that at St. Peters there may be about 200 men in scatter'd houses, and in the suburbs of the Town of Louisbourg without the Walls about 200. it is improbable that more than two 30 or 40 Gun ships should come with Mr. Duviver who may be expected the first with Recruits & supplies, and in case the naval Force that comes should be superiour to our naval Force, that our 3000 men would command the Field, & continue so till they could be protected & Reinforc'd from England.

Indorsed, "Cape Britton

Exped^n—Plan of operation, Feby 1, 1745—"

His Exc^y sent down ye following written Message by Coll. Downing & Mr. Solly:

Gentlemen of the Assembly,

In consequence of your message of the 2^d Inst. I express'd a messenger to Boston in order to get the Proclamations necessary to be Dispersed throughout the Province for encouraging the Expedition to Louisburgh printed, which I have this moment received, & as soon as the sheriff attends on me shall order them to be dispersed.

B. WENTWORTH.

Council Chamber, In Portsm° Feby 5th 1745.

Message of His Excellency.

Gentlemen of the Assembly,

By your message of this day, I find the disposition of the House is to augment the forces to Louisburgh to four or five hundred men, sailors included, which is very pleasing to me; and if the House will send up a Resolve on that subject & in what manner they propose to pay the Expence, it will facilitate the other bill that now lays before me, which at present appears very difficult;—but by no means put off the augmentation or the charge to a further day.

Council Chamber in   B. WENTWORTH.
Portsm° Feby 12, 1745—

February 14, 1745, Mr. Secretary came down with the following Message from his Exc^y: His Ex^cy recomends it to the House to pass a vote that the officers & soldiers in y^s Province for the Expedition ag^st Louisburg have ye same pay as in the Massachusetts, wch he apprehends would be for the encouraging the affairs going on.

Voted That the Collonel, Lt. Collonel & Major, Captains & all under officers that are or shall be appointed to command the voluntiers voted by the Genl Assembly to go on the Expedition ag^st Louisburg have the same allowances made them pr month as are allowed by the Government of the Mass: Bay on ye s^d Expedition, provided each Company consists of forty men or upwards, & that the Captains have the same allowance for enlisting men in proportion to the number of men in each Company & that no Capt. be entitled to the bounty for enlisting men untill his Company be compleated;

Voted, That the same encouragement be given to private Centinalls & sailors that will enlist as voluntiers on ye Exped^n ag^st Louisburgh as is given in ye Prov. of Mass^a Bay,

Establishment of the officers' Pay in Massachusetts on the Expedition against Louisbourgh, 1745.

Generall pr month	£15 :
Collonell	12
Lt. Coll	10
Major	8
Adjutant	4 : 10
Capt.	4 : 10
Lieut	3
2ᵈ Lieut	2
Sergent	1 : 10
Corporal	1 : 8
Clerk	4
Surgeon Genⁿ	5
Under Surgeon	4 : 10
Drum Major	1 : 12
Comon Drumʳ	1
Chaplain	4 : 10
Capt of yᵉ Artillery	9
Lieut	4 : 10
Qr. Gunner	2
2 Bombarders	4
Do Assistance	1 : 12
Armorer	1 : 12

Incouragement for the men that Inlist, viz.

To each man besides what is mentioned in the Proclamation by way of Bounty, old Tenor,	£4 :
To Billiting money from the Time of Inlisting pr. week to pay from the time of Inlisting	1 :
To each Capt. over & above his pay for his Expences in Visiting his Company, old Tenʳ	25 :

Further to Incourage men to Inlist it is proposed that the Widows or nearest relatives of any offcer or soldier

that is slain or shall otherwise loose his life in the service,
shall be entitled to four months pay.

And that the wives of any officer or soldier in the Expedition or any other person that appears with a power of
Attorney duly authenticated, shall at the end of every
month receive out of the Treasury half or all the wages of
such officer or soldier as he appears for which will greatly
encourage the present Expedition.

Boston Feby 26, 1745.

Sir—

I am extremely glad to hear of your good prospect of
completing your Regiment in time: All things will be
ready here for the Imbarcation of our fleet by the end of
the week as the committee informs me, so I should be glad
of your being ready with yours as soon as may be; whatever you want for the 150 men to go wth my commissions
& in the pay of this government, be pleased to send to me
for it by Express and you shall have it instantly.

I think the essential thing is the number of men in the
whole; and y^t it is not absolutely necessary y^t there should
be exactly 50 men in each company, if there are 40 in one
and 60 in another, all the things may be set right by pro-
portioning the service in the field; and indeed if a company does not consist of less y^n 40 men I think we ought
not to be critical.

I am wth much & respect

y^r Excelencys most

Obedient humble servant

W. SHIRLEY.

His Exc^y. Govr Wentworth.

Boston, March 27, 1745.

Sir—

I should have mentioned y^t this morning Donahoe sail'd
with another sloop under his convoy having on board a
company of 50 men to reconnoitre the Coast, &c. and to

clear it agst the arrival of the Fleet, and if it should happen y^t your Transports should get the start of ours, I am advis'd y^t it would be safest for 'em to stop at Whitehead Harbour ab^t 5 or 6 Leagues short of Canso, till the arrival of ours y^t there may be as little danger as is possible of occasioning intelligence being convey'd to the Enemy by any little vessell to the Eastward of Canso, wch may discover 'em; and if you approve of it I shall be glad if you order it accordingly. I am inform'd y^t Mr. Sparhawk has got some very good cutlasses and some firelocks wch it is doubted are not extraordinary: If you will be pleas'd to take the trouble of appointing some skillfull person to view both of 'em, and in case they or either of 'em are approv'd of, desire him to put such as are approv'd on board one of your Transports for the use of our Troops as spare arms, I shall be oblig'd to you, and our Committee will pay him for 'em. But if they are not good I would not have 'em. We forgot to put up among the Stores for our 150 men in your Regiment Gunpowder and Ball: If you will be pleas'd to supply 'em with three half barrels of powder and a like proportion of Ball for their passage, I shall be oblig'd to you, and will repay you by the first opportunity; The Blankets and money not used be pleas'd to return by a convenient opportunity. I must beg the favour of you to indulge Mr. Bollan in his Inclos'd request, if no inconvenience will attend it. I have so much fatigue y^t I wth great difficulty hold out, but not without having impair'd my health.

God send us both a good riddance of our Trouble and an happy Event to the Expedition.

I am sincerely,

Your Exc^{ys} faithfull, humble servant

W. SHIRLEY.

To his Exc^y Gov. Wentworth.

2

Boston May–13–1745

Sir

As to the agreement your Excellency mentions to be made between you and me, that the Companies to be rais'd in your Government should consist of 40 men each, and that three companys of 50 men each should at all Events be rais'd by you to be in the pay of this Government & added to your companies, I am apt to think may be a mistake.

It is certain that I always intended and understood the agreement to be that you should if you pleas'd raise as many men to be in the pay of this Province as would make up your 350 a Regiment of 500 men.

I can't pretend to recollect every expression which may have dropped from my pen on this affair between us; But I am satisfied the agreement you mention is so foreign to my intention that upon perusing my letters again and comparing 'em with your own you will find the real agreement to be, that all the men not exceeding 150 to be raised by you over and above the Quota of 350 Voted by your Assembly, should be paid and subsisted by this Government. The reason of my mentioning to you the vote of the Assembly of this Province for reducing our Companies from 50 men in each to 40, was to remove the difficulty of their first vote which I was afraid might ly in your way as it did in mine here, by which no Captain that had not raised 50 men was entituled to have his Company received into pay; whereas by the second vote fourty men was to be received as a Company, which I found an ease to me in raiseing my own Levies, but whatever I have said in that respect was not designed in the least as a proposal or agreement that your Companys should be only eight in number and consist of no more than 40 men Each, and that at all events this Province was to pay & subsist 150 men of New Hampshire Regiment. But upon the whole I ever understood that this Government was to pay and sub-

sist as many men not exceeding 150 as you should raise
within your Province over and above your own Govern-
ments Quota of 350 & no more.

    I am with great respect

        Sir—your Excellencys most obedient

                humble servant

                    W. SHIRLEY.

His Exc^y Govr Wentworth.

The New Hampshire Adjutant-General's Report, Vol. 2,
1866, contains the rolls of the seven companies in Colonel
Moore's regiment, over his own signature, dated at Louisburg, November 20, 1745. The adjutant-general quotes
Dr. Belknap, as follows:

"Thus, Dr. Belknap states that Col. Moore's regiment
consisted of eight companies, when the return of his regiment, over his own signature, shows but seven companies."

We think the following letter of Governor Wentworth
will show the eighth company, as it was one of the companies not returned by Colonel Moore.

---

*Letter from His Excellency Benning Wentworth, Esq., Gov-
ernor of New Hampshire, to Lt. General Pepperell.*

                        March 23^d 1745.

SR.

    I herewith transmitt to you a List of the Transports
employ'd by this Government for the service of the Expedition against the French at Louisburg, also what Transports are employ'd to transport the one hundred & fifty
men, in the pay of the Massachusetts Government, which
are aggregated to the Regiment, whereof I have appointed
Saml Moore, Esq. Colonel. Also I think proper to acquaint
you that I have appointed Capt. Fernald Commander of a
Sloop fitted out by this Government, in a warlike manner,
to annoy his Majesty's Enemies, and to guard and convoy

the Transports. I have also appointed the said Jn° Fernald a Capt of a Company in Col. Moore's Regiment to act either by Land or by sea, as the service may require it. I have thought it necessary, in order to preserve the Command you are appointed to, that you have the intire command and disposition of the Regiment and Transports, also of the Sloop of War, And I do hereby put the same absolutely under your command, hereby requiring them to obey you, as their Commander-in-Chief, and to follow such orders and commands as from time to time they or either of them shall receive from you.

Sr—yʳ Hum : servᵗ

B. WENTWORTH.

Lieutenant-general William Pepperell, of Kittery, Me., was commander-in-chief of the land forces, sailors, and marines on board the transports and the armed vessels that convoyed the troops to Louisburg—the total number of men, probably 4,000, and all furnished by the provinces of New Hampshire, Massachusetts, Connecticut, and Rhode Island.*

Governor Wentworth's proclamation for enlisting soldiers and sailors for the Louisburg expedition not on record, or copy known to be in existence.

Off for Louisburg.

After two months' discussion of measures by the Assembly and Council, then in session at Portsmouth, to raise men and money to defray expenses, the expedition was ready, and sailed from Portsmouth March 23ᵈ O. S., or April 4ᵗʰ N. S., 1745—several days before the Massachusetts troops left Boston. The New Hampshire regiment was 500 strong, under the command of Col. Samuel Moore, of Portsmouth; eight companies, and probably three com-

*Did not arrive at Louisburg until after the fort was captured.

panies (150 men) of New Hampshire in the pay of Massachusetts, in Colonel Moore's regiment. On this point
there has been a wide diversity of opinion, as there is not,
as far as is now known, a single muster or pay-roll in
existence. It was customary at that time in the English
service for the field officers to have command of companies
as colonel and captain at the same time. In order to sub-
stantiate my view that there were eleven companies in
Colonel Moore's regiment, of 45 men to each company, the
names of all the commissioned officers, date of commission,
and date of discharge, are given, all the others being
recruits, after the capture of Louisburg, June 17, 1745.

Names.	Rank.	Date of Commission.	Date of Discharge.
Moore, Samuel,	Colonel.	Feb. 12, 1745.	Aug. 15, 1746.
Meserve, Nathaniel, 2d,	Colonel.	Feb. 13, 1745.	Nov. 11, 1745.
Gilman, Ezekiel,	Major.	Feb. 13, 1745.	Nov. 11, 1745.
*Mason, John T.,	Captain.	Feb. 13, 1745.	July 31, 1745.
Seaward, William,	Captain.	Feb. 13, 1745.	Nov. 10, 1745.
†Fernald, John,	Captain.	Feb. 13, 1745.	Nov. 11, 1745.
Sherburne, Henry,	Captain.	Feb. 13, 1745.	June 28, 1745.
Ladd, Daniel,	Captain.	Feb. 13, 1745.	Sept. 4, 1745.
‡Hale, Samuel,	Captain.	Feb. 13, 1745.	July 15, 1746.
Whidden, James,	Captain.	Feb. 13, 1745.	Nov. 10, 1745.
Waldron, Thomas W.,	Captain.	Feb. 13, 1745.	Sept. 6, 1745.
Dudley, Trueworthy,	Captain.	Feb. 13, 1745.	July 21, 1745.
Tilton, Jacob,	Captain.	March 1, 1745.	Nov. 11, 1745.
Williams, Edward,	Captain.	March 2, 1745.	Feb. 6, 1746.
§Wise, John,	Captain.	April 15, 1745.	No date.
Sherburne, Joseph,	Captain.	June 6, 1745.	June 30, 1746.

Lieutenants.

Names.	Rank.	Date of Commission.	Date of Discharge.
Hart, John,	Lieutenant.	Feb. 13, 1745.	July 31, 1745.
Leavett, Samuel,	Lieutenant.	Feb. 13, 1745.	Sept. 6, 1745.
White, Samuel,	Lieutenant.	Feb. 13, 1745.	Oct. 9, 1745.
‖Flagg, John,	Lieutenant.	Feb. 13, 1745.	Sept. 30, 1745.

* No company; independent command.
† Captain of armed sloop Abigail.
‡ Promoted to major Oct. 16, 1745.
§ Captain of armed sloop.
‖ Promoted to captain. No date.

Daniels, Eliphalet,	Lieutenant.	Feb. 13, 1745.	July 31, 1745.
Foss, Zachariah,	Lieutenant.	Feb. 13, 1745.	Nov. 14, 1745.
Wheelwright, Jeremiah,	Lieutenant.	Feb. 13, 1745.	Sept. 22, 1745.
Dudley, James,	Lieutenant.	Feb. 13, 1745.	Aug. 7, 1745.
Wingate, Moses,	Lieutenant.	Feb. 13, 1745.	Sept. 30, 1745.
Mattoon, Richard,	Lieutenant.	Feb. 13, 1745.	Nov. 11, 1745.
Robie, Samuel,	Lieutenant.	Feb. 13, 1745.	Sept. 30, 1745.
Connor, Samuel,	Lieutenant.	Feb. 13, 1745.	July 31, 1745.

Ensigns.

Names.	Rank.	Date of Commission.	Date of Discharge.
*Newmarch, Thomas,	Ensign.	Feb. 13, 1745.	June 20, 1746.
†Brown, Edmund,	Ensign.	Feb. 13, 1745.	July 1, 1746.
Tufts, Thomas,	Ensign.	Feb. 13, 1745.	Sept. 6, 1745.
Wormall, Daniel,	Ensign.	Feb. 13, 1745.	Nov. 11, 1745.
‡Pitman, Ezekiel, Jr.,	Ensign.	Feb. 13, 1745.	Nov. 10, 1745.
Huntress, Christopher,	Ensign.	Feb. 13, 1745.	July 31, 1745.
Brooks, Edward,	Ensign.	Feb. 13, 1745.	July 31, 1745.
Pickerin, Thomas,	Ensign.	Feb. 13, 1745.	Aug. 7, 1745.
Sleeper, Joseph,	Ensign.	Feb. 13, 1745.	Sept. 22, 1745.
Ham, Clement,	Ensign.	Feb. 13, 1745.	Sept. 30, 1745.
Perkins, Robert,	Ensign.	Feb. 13, 1745.	July 31, 1745.

The above-named officers were commissioned by Benning Wentworth, the governor of the province of New Hampshire.

Lieutenant-general Pepperell, at Canso, April 15, commissioned Abraham Trefethen, captain; Jonathan Gilman, lieutenant; Philip Yeaton, ensign.

Recruits.

Friday–June–8–1745.

The House met according to adjournment.

Voted, That Eleaz[r] Russel Esq. Mr. Henry Sherburne jun. & Tho[s] Bell Esq. be a Com[tee] of this House to join with such as may be appointed by y[e] Hon[ble] Council to consider of y[e] subject matter of his Excel[y] Gov[r] Shirly & Lieut. Gen[l] Pepperells Letters relating to a Reinforcement

---

* Promoted to lieutenant Oct. 5.
† Promoted to lieutenant Oct. 1.
‡ Promoted to lieutenant June 20.

of our army at Louisburg & to consider what is proper for
this Province to do & to make Report to the Gen¹ Court as
soon as may be.

The Com^{tee} for considering the subject matter of his
Exc^y Govr Shirlys & Lieut Gen¹ Pepperrells Letters relating a Reinforcement of the Army before Louisburgh,
report as follows:

The Com^{tee} are humbly of opinion that (when proper
methods may be agreed upon by the Gen¹ Assembly for
defraying the charge) his Exc^y the Capt. Gen¹ be desired
to issue forth his Proclamation for the Encouraging the
enlisting of one hundred voluntiers under such proper
officers as he may think proper to be employ'd in the
Expedition against Louisburgh giving them the same
Encouragement as was given to ye last voluntiers inlisted
for said Expedition.

| Prov. of
N. Hampr | In ye House of Represent June
10th 1745, Read and accepted &
sent up for concurrence | Jotham Odiorn
R. Wibird
Saml Solly
Eleazr Russell
Hen. Sherburne
Thos Bell | Com-
mittee |

Wednesday June 12th 1745.

The House met according to adjournment.

Mr. Secretary Atkinson came into the House & inform
them that ye vote on Louisburgh Expedition, Com^{tees}
Report for one Hund^d men were concurr'd & assented to
by the Governor.

Tuesday July 2^d 1745.

The House met according to adjournment.

Mr. Secretary bro't into ye House a written message
from his Excellency representing the Probability of 20 men
being raised more than are voted for & Desiring to know
whether ye House would have them Embark'd &c. and
then the House adjourned for two Hours.

His Excellency's Message.

Gentlemen of the Assembly

It is very probable that about twenty men more than what are voted to be raised for the reinforcement of our troops now before Louisburgh, may appear, in which case I shall be glad to have your Resolve whether it will not be expedient to Imbark them, as it will greatly relieve the Forces now there from the hard duty they have so long undergone.

I shall also be glad to have your mind signified whether it be your Intent to have the Reinforcement Imbarked in case news should arrive before Imbarkation of the reduction of Louisburgh.

B. WENTWORTH.

Council Chamber in
Portsmouth, July 2d, 1745.

Saturday July 6ᵗʰ 1745.

Met according to adjournment.

In answer to his Excllʳˢ message by Mr. Secretary to know yᵉ opinion of yᵉ House about sending the Reinforcement for the army at Cape Britton & whether if twenty men more than yᵉ hundred appear'd the House were willing they should be sent,

Voted, That the Reinforcement be sent away with all possible Dispatch & that if twenty men more or any smaller number appeared as voluntiers they also be sent with them at the publick expense.

Statement of the Condition of the Men at Louisburg, 1745.

To His Excellency the Governor, the Honorable the Council, and House of Representatives, of His Majesties Province of New Hampshire.—

As we are refer'd to, in the preceeding Memorial, to give further Information, touching the State of our Soldiers; and authorized thereby, to Sollicit the Honorable Court in their behalf; we humbly crave Leave, to offer this, as a Supplement thereto.—

Besides the almost Naked Condition of those of our Troops, who went first to Cape Breton; Some of them are So enfeebled, by reason of the Length and Hardships of the Siege, & for want of necessary Comforts, in the Time of it, as renders them unfit for further Service, till Recruited; others are Languishing under Sicknesses, of Various kinds, and most of them, are overrun with Lice, for want of Change of Apparel, which renders their Case still more uncomfortable, Whereupon, we humbly recommend, those Poor but brave men, to your Excellency's & Honour's wise, Just, and Compassionate Consideration, Earnestly beseeching, that Such of them as desire it, may be immediatly dismiss'd, and bro't back to their Native Country, their Families, & Friends; that it may never be Said, they bravely fought themselves into a Prison; for, what Else can be Said of it If they are Compell'd to tarry, after the Expedition is Ended, as we apprehend it is, and that in a most Compleat and effectual Manner: For that, His Excellencys Proclamation of the 2 of February Last, proposed an Expedition, for the Reduction of the French Settlements, on the Island of Cape Breton, & not for the garrisoning of them; and the Enlistment, was in Consequence thereof, (namely,) for Reducing, & not for garrisoning, and we humbly appeal, to your Excellency's & Honors Judgment, whether, reducing and garrisoning, be not two things, quite different, and Distinct from each other; and if so, whether the Troops of the first Embarkation, mayn't demand a discharge, as a Right and Justice due to them, instead of Solliciting for it, as an Act of Grace. But, on the other hand, if it Should be Said, that by the Expedition was meant and intended, that Louisbourg Should be garrison'd (in case of Success,) by those who should reduce it; It may be Answer'd, that Such Intention, cant Rationally be Extended further, than till

other Troops, might be rais'd to relieve them ; and more
than three Months, is already Pass'd, Since the Surrender;
a Space doubly Sufficient for that Purpose.—

We take Leave further to Propose, that in Consideration,
the Plunder (which was expected would be great,) turns
out, to be but a very Triffle, they May have an additional
Grant of Bounty, as a further Reward, of their Toil, Haz-
ard, and Bravery, as the Massachusetts Troops have already had.—

As to those, whose Lot may be to tarry over the Winter,
Whether by Choice, or Compulsion, (if any Should be
Compell'd so to Do,) We humbly propose, that besides an
Augmentation of their Wages, and a Grant of Apparell,
and Bedding, Suitable for the Climate and Season ; they
May have an Augmentation of their allowance of Rum &
Molasses, to half a Pint of Each, for Each Man ℔ Day,
and a Couple of Quarts of Small Beer also, the Waters
there, being exceeding bad, and very unwholesome to
Drink : that there may be a Surplus of Stores, of all kinds,
to be Purchased of the Commissary, at a Stated Price, and
that there may be a Provision of Physic, as well as of Food
& Cloathing; and that Each Capᵗ may have a Copy, of the
Invoices of the Stores & Cloaths Sent for the Soldiers, with
the Prices of those Commodities, that they may be Sent
for Sale ; that the Care, the Justice, & the goodness of the
Honorable Court, may be made known to every individual
Man.—

As the Season of the year is far advanced, and the Soldiers greatly distress'd ; Some For Want of a Discharge,
and other for want of Necessarys and Conveniences, to
make their Lives Comfortable, We humbly Pray, that what
we have offered, may have the earliest Consideration &
Dispatch, that is Possible.

And your Memorialists as in Duty bound Shall Ever
Pray

                                        T. W. Waldron
Portsmouth Sepᵗ 24 1745   Jonathan Prescut

Miscellaneous.—Notes, prior to, during, and after the Siege of Louisbury.

It appears from Gov. Wentworth's proclamation, or enlistment papers to the captains, for the enlisting of soldiers, and sailors, no particular time was inserted for their discharge, after the surrender of the fortress, the men were clamorous for their discharge, and not being complied with, caused considerable trouble, some of them were held until the arrival of troops from Great Britain, May 24, 1746, when 1500 were released.

The Louisburg expedition cost the province of New Hampshire, as reported by a committee of the Assembly, June 3, 1747, 26,489 pounds, 16 shillings, 8½ pence, Proclamation money.

Great Britain reimbursed the Province of New Hampshire, 16,355 pounds sterling. The money arrived in Boston, Sept. 18, 1749. The British fleet, commanded by Commodore Peter Warren, arrived before Louisburg at the commencement of hostilities, with the following vessels of war :

Superb	60	guns.
Launceston	40	"
Mermaid	40	"
*—Vigilant	64	"
May 22—Princes Mary	60	"
" "—Hector	40	"
June 10—Chester	50	"
" 12—Canterbury	60	"
" "—Sunderland	60	"
" "—Lark	40	"
" "—Eltham	40	"

This immense fleet of vessels of war took no active part in the assaults on the fortress, with the exception of a few

*Captured from the French, and manned by New England sailors.

gunners, who went ashore to instruct Pepperell's men in the management of their batteries.

Capt. Edward Tyng was in command of the Massachusetts Colonial squadron of seven vessels, carrying 108 guns.

Capt. John Fernald, of Portsmouth, commanded the sloop Abigail, of 14 guns, that convoyed the New Hampshire troops.

Two sloops from Connecticut, 30 guns, one armed vessel from Rhode Island, 20 guns,* with one hundred and fifty soldiers.

Belknap's History of New Hampshire.

"The fortress of Louisburg was so strong as to called, The Dunkirk of America ; and had been twenty-five years in building, and cost 1,200,000 pounds Sterling.

"This expedition originated in Massachusetts, but the colonies of New Hampshire, Rhode Island, and Connecticut by their legislative authority, furnished troops and stores, New York sent a supply of artillery, Pennsylvania, and New Jersey, provisions and clothing." The assault on the Island battery, defended by 180 men, and 30 cannon, was disastrous to the 400 provincial troops who made the assault, nearly one half being either killed, drowned, or taken prisoners.

The French loss during the entire siege, is reported to have been 200 men.

When Duchambon, the Governor of Cape Breton, surrendered to Generel Pepperell, there was turned over to him, 1,900 prisoners, 125 large cannon, 19 mortars, stores of provisions, enough to last six months.

General Amherst, commanding the land forces, and Admiral Boscawen, of the British navy, captured Louisburg, July 26, 1758, and completely destroyed the splendid fortress, and it remains so to this date.

No enumeration of the number of the inhabitants of New Hampshire, was made until 1767, when there were 52,700.

*Did not arrive in Louisburg until after the fortress was taken.

The ratable polls returned in 1742 as 5,172, with Nottingham, Barrington, and Gosport, missing. Call the number of ratable polls in 1745, 6,000, and multiply by 4.50, would give the number of inhabitants in New Hampshire in 1745 as 27,000.

France declared war against Great Britain March 15, 1744, N. S.

Great Britain declared war against France, March 29, 1744, O. S.

After the treaty of peace, October 7, 1748, Louisburg was turned over to the French intact, and the British troops evacuated Louisburg July 12, 1749. And the provinces gained practically nothing for their blood and treasure expended during the war.

The pay of the soldiers in provincial currency was twenty-five shillings a month, or less than sixpence a day, sterling, the soldier furnishing his own clothing and gun.

From Parkman's, "A Half Century of Conflict":

"The New England soldier fancied that he was doing the work of God. And the descendant of the Puritans was never so well pleased as when teaching their duty to other people, whether by pen, voice, or bombshells. The ragged artillerymen, battering the walls of papistical Louisburg, flattered themselves with the notion that they were champions of gospel truth. Barefoot and tattered, they toiled on with indomitable pluck, doing the work which oxen could not do, with no comfort but their daily dram of New England rum."

"Maine, then a part of Massachusetts, furnished full one third of the men of the Massachusetts contingent."

According to Parkman, the winter of 1746 must have been terrible, on account of sickness, "At the end of January, five hundred, and sixty one had died"

"On May 10, 1746, Governor Shirley writes to Newcastle, that eight hundred and ninety men, had died during the winter"

From Douglas, North America:

" outside the Maurepas Gate, by the old lime-Kiln, the forgotten bones of above five hundred New England men lie there to this day, under the coarse neglected grass "

There is in the library of the New Hampshire Historical society at Concord, a book containing two hundred and sixty pages, inscribed as follows : " A List of Prisoners tryed at General Court Martial held at Louisburg, in the Island of Cape Breton, in the years 1746—1747 & 1748." And has the appearance of being, and undoubtedly is, the original journal.

The officers of the New Hampshire troops on their return home, presented a bell (which has since been re-cast) that they had captured at Louisburg, to Queen's Chapel, Portsmouth. The peal of the brazen-tongued messenger from the grim old fortifications of Louisburg is still heard from the tower of St John's church.

From Barstow's History of New Hampshire :

" Louisburg was situated on a neck of land south of one of the finest harbors on the island. The city was surrounded by a wall of stone thirty-six feet high."

William Vaughan of Portsmouth is said to have been the originator of the Louisburg expedition.

Not a man in the expedition had previously seen Louisburg.

Distance from Portsmouth to Louisburg about six hundred miles.

The city of Louisburg, at the time of its capture, contained 5,000 inhabitants, exclusive of the troops.

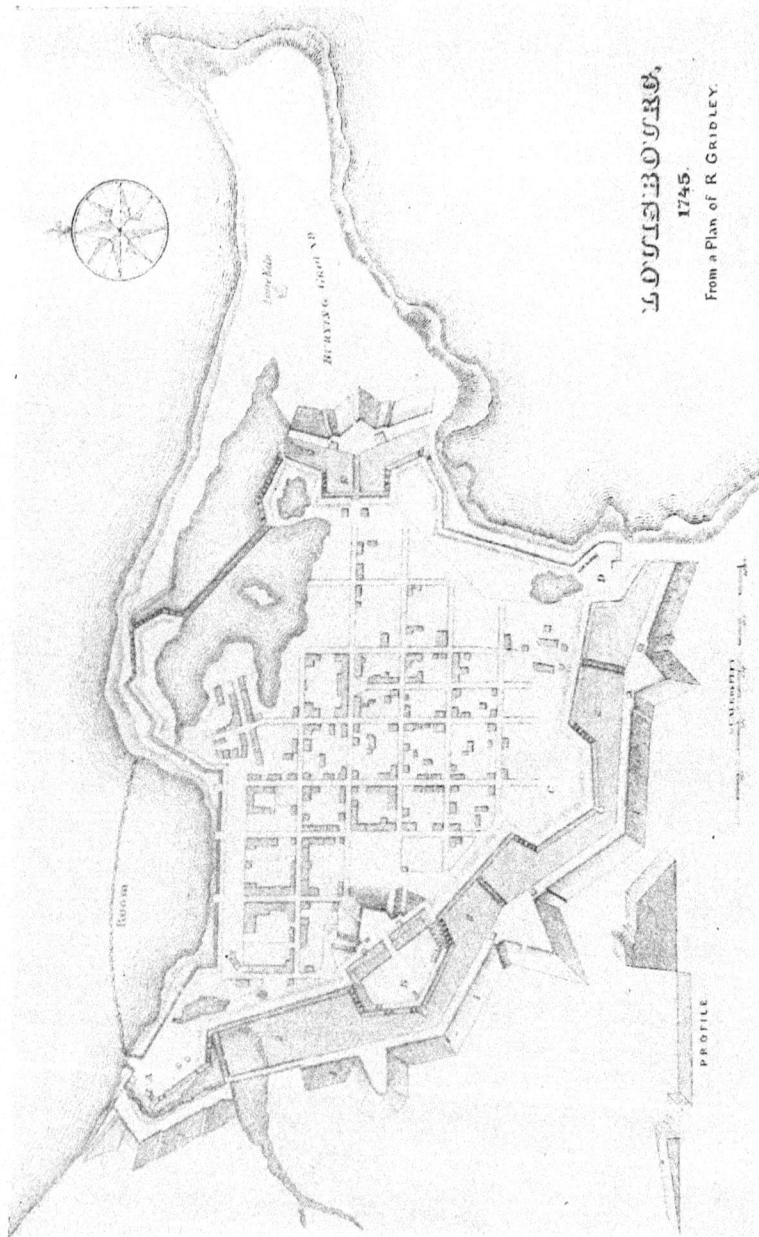

LOUISBOURG,
1745.
From a Plan of R. GRIDLEY.

BURYING GROUND

PROFILE

From "A Half Century of Conflict," by Francis Parkman.

INDEX

TO PLAN OF LOUISBOURG, 1745.

From a Survey by Lieutenant-Colonel R. Gridley.

A Dauphin's Bastion and West Gate.
B King's Bastion, or Citadel.
C Queen's Bastion.
D Princess's Bastion and South Gate.
E Maurepas Bastion and East Gate.
1111 Glacis.
222 Ditch.

NEW HAMPSHIRE MEN IN THE LOUISBURG EXPEDITION, 1745.

NAMES.	Residence.	Enlisted.	Rank.	Company.	Reg't.
Atkinson, John.........	....	Feb. 13	Private	Moore's....	Moore's.
Ackers, Joseph	Exeter.........	....	"	Light's.....	"
Addison, Jonas	....	....	"	"	"
Atkinson, Joseph......	Brentwood	....	"	"	"
Adams, John..........	Londonderry..	June 20	"	Sherburne's	"
Ambrose, Jonathan....	Exeter.........	....	"	"	"
Aylmer, Valentine.....	....	....	"	"	"
Abbott, Joseph........	Dover..........	Feb. 13	"	Hale's	"
Allen, Daniel..........	Greenland.....	....	"	Whidden's.	"
Abbott, John..........	....	....	"	....	"
[1] Allcock, John	Portsmouth....	Feb. 13	"	....	"
Arickson, Samuel......	....	....	"	....	"
Barker, John.........	....	Feb. 13	"	Moore's....	"
Black, Adam	....	....	"	"	"
Blake, John, Jr.......··	Kensington....	"	Corp.	"	"
[1] Broughton, Noah	Portsmouth....	"	Private	"	"
Brown, Isaac.........	....	"	"	"	"
Batt, Thomas	....	....	Sergt.	Fellows's ..	"
Bell, Timothy........	....	....	Private	"	"
Bickford, Jethro.......	Newington	......·....	"	"	"
Boothby, Jonathan....	Portsmouth....	....	"	"	"
Brewster, Richard.....	"	....	"	"	"
Brown, Caleb	Brentwood	....	"	Light's.....	"
Brown, John	"	....	"	"	"
Boardman, John	....	Feb. 13	"	Sherburne's	"
Blake, Samuel	Kensington....	....	"	Prescott's..	"
Bean, Edward.........	....	....	"	Hale's	"
Bean, Nathaniel	....	Feb. 13	"	"	"
Berry, Joseph........	....	"	"	"	"
[2] Bunker, Benjamin	Durham.......	"	"	"	"
Buss, Joseph..........	Dover.......	"	"	"	"
Bussell, Jacob	"	"	"	"	"
Bussell, John	"	"	Sergt.	"	"
Bond, Jonathan	....	"	Private	Williams's.	"
Blake, Timothy.......	Hampton Falls	"	Private	Williams's.	"
[3] Brown, Edmund	Hampton Falls	"	Ensign	"	"
Bennett, Abraham	....	....	Private	Whidden's.	"
Brewster, John	....	....	"	"	"
Barber, Joseph	....	April 15	"	Trefethen's	"
Blake, Josiah	....	....	"	"	"
Bassett, Richard......	....	....	"	....	"
Bean, Daniel	Kingston	Feb. 13	"	....	"
Bickford, Eleazer.. ...	Durham.......	"	"	....	"
Blake, Samuel, Jr......	Kensington....	....	"	....	"
[4] Blaster, Joseph	....	....	Mariner	....	"
Brooks, Edward	Portsmouth....	Feb. 13	Ensign	....	"
Buntin, Samuel	....	....	Private	....	"
Center, Abraham	....	....	"	Fellows's ..	"
Claridge, Thomas	....	....	"	"	"
Colbath, Pitman	Newmarket....	....	"	"	"
Colbath, Joseph	....	..........·	"	"	"
Colbath, Benjamin.....	Newington	....	"	"	"
Cooper, Jonathan	....	....	"	"	"
Cooper, John.........	....	....	"	"	"
Cloyd, James	Brentwood	....	"	Light's.....	"
Coney, Jack..........	....	....	"	"	"
Creighton, George.....	Exeter.........	....	"	"	"
Carter, John..........	Londonderry..	June 20	"	Sherburne's	"
Cass, Abner	....	....	"	"	"
Cotton, John	Portsmouth....	Feb. 13	Sergt.	"	"
Cunningham, Robert ..	Londonderry..	June 20	Private	"	"
Chapman, John	Kensington....	....	"	Prescott's..	"
Chase, Enoch	....	....	"	"	"

[1] Taken prisoner. [2] Promoted to Ensign Aug. 10. [3] Promoted to Lieutenant Oct. 1. [4] Killed.

NEW HAMPSHIRE MEN IN THE LOUISBURG EXPEDITION, 1745.—*Cont.*

NAMES.	Residence.	Enlisted.	Rank.	Company.	Reg't.
Challis, Thomas			Private	Prescott's..	Moore's.
Choate, Jonathan	Kingston		"	"	"
Clifford, William	"		"	"	"
Cram, Benjamin			"	"	"
Cash, Thomas	Dover	Feb. 13	"	Hale,s	"
Clark, Josiah			"	"	"
Clark, Stephen			"	"	"
Cook, Ebenezer	Dover		"	"	"
Critchet, James			"	"	"
Calfe, Robert	Chester		Sergt.	Williams's.	"
Cass, Nason	Exeter		Private	"	"
Cram, Daniel	Hampton Falls		"	"	"
Cucknet, William			"	Whidden's.	"
Cummin, Benjamin			"	Trefethen's	"
Card, Edward	Newcastle	Feb. 13	Mariner	Fernald's..	"
Card, Thomas	"		"	"	"
Colby, Spencer	Portsmouth	"	"	"	"
Crimble, Charles			"		"
Carty, John			Private		"
[1] Cass, Jonathan	Kensington	Feb. 13	"		"
Clark, Alexander		Oct. 17	Surgeon		"
Conner, Samuel		Feb. 13	Lieut.		"
[2] Cotton, Timothy	Portsmouth	"	Private		"
Dalton, Benjamin		"	"	Moore's	"
Dunkin, John		"	"	"	"
Dam, Jonathan			"	Fellows's..	"
Downing, Joseph			"	"	"
Dunn, Thomas			"	"	"
Dolloff, Amos	Exeter		"	Light's	"
Dolloff, David	"		"	"	"
Dudley, Joseph			"	"	"
Dudley, Joseph, Jr			"	"	"
Davis, Moses			"	Prescott's..	"
Davis, William			"	"	"
Dow, Charles			"	"	"
Dow, Nathan	Kensington		"	"	"
Dam, William	Dover		"	Hale's	"
Daniels, David	"		"	"	"
Drew, Zebulon	"		"	"	"
Durgin, William			"	"	"
[3] Dudley, Trueworthy	Exeter	Feb. 13	Capt.	Dudley's ..	"
[4] Daniels, Eliphalet	Durham	"	Lieut.	Fernald's..	"
Doe, Daniel	"	"	Mariner	"	"
Daniels, Benjamin		Apr. 15	"	Trefethen's	"
Davison, Dudley		"	"		"
Dam, George	Portsmouth	Feb. 13	Private		"
Dam, Waymouth			"		"
Dam, Theophilus	Newington	Feb. 13	"		"
Dacker, David	Portsmouth	"	"		"
Dearborn, Shubael	Hampton		"		"
Dent, John	Kingston		"		"
Denerson, John	Portsmouth		"		"
Dolloff, John			Sergt.		"
Dow, Jeremiah	Hampton		Private		"
Downer, Andrew			Officer		"
[5] Dudley, James	Exeter	Feb. 13	Lieut.		"
[6] Dunn, Nicholas	Portsmouth	"	Private		"
[7] Emery, Anthony	Hampton	"	Surgeon		"
Elliot, Abraham			Private	Fellows's ..	Moore's.
Edgerly, John			"	Light's	"
Ealet, John			"	Prescott's	"
Eastman, Samuel			"	"	"
Evans, Stephen	Dover	Feb. 13	"	Hale's	"

[1] Died Sept. 13, 1745.   [2] Taken prisoner.   [3] Discharged July 21.   [4] Wounded
and prisoner.   [5] Discharged Aug. 7.   [6] Killed.   [7] Mass. Artillery Co.

3

NEW HAMPSHIRE MEN IN THE LOUISBURG EXPEDITION, 1745.—*Cont.*

Names.	Residence.	Enlisted.	Rank.	Company.	Reg't.
Ellest, John			Private	Williams's.	Moore's.
Emery, Daniel			"	Whidden's.	"
Edgerly, Samuel	Brentwood	Feb. 13	"		"
Eyre, John	Portsmouth	"	Adjt.		"
Ficket, John	"	"	Private	Moore's	"
1 Flagg, John	"	"	Lieut.	"	"
2 Flagg, John, Jr	"	"	Private	"	"
Forham, Richard		"	"	"	"
3 Fellows, Nathaniel		June 20	Lieut.	Fellows's	"
Fitzgerald, Richard			Private	"	"
Foy, John	Dover		"	"	"
Furber, Richard	Newington		"	"	"
Ferrin, Moses			"	Light's	"
Fifield, William			"	"	"
Flanders, Moses			"	"	"
Folsom, Joseph			"	"	"
Forrest, John			"	"	"
Fellows, John			"	Prescott's	"
Ferrel, John	Somersworth	Feb. 13	"	Hale's	"
Folsom, John	"	"	"	"	"
Forse, John	Dover		"	"	"
Fowler, Morrice	"	"	"	"	"
Fox, Edward	Newmarket	"	"	"	"
4 French, John	Hampton Falls	"	"	Williams's.	"
5 Fernald, John	Portsmouth	"	Capt.	Fernald's	"
Foss, Zachariah		"	Lieut.	"	"
Furbush, Benjamin	Dover		Private	Wise's	"
Furguson, John			"		"
Fales, Nathan			"		"
6 Folsom, Jonathan :		June 17	Lieut.		"
Frost, Samuel	Portsmouth		Private		"
Fullerton, William	Brentwood		"		"
Gooding, David		Feb. 13	"	Moore's	"
Gordon, David		"	"	"	"
Green, John		"	"	"	"
Gardner, Joseph			"	Light's	"
Gibson, John			"	"	"
Giles, Joseph	Brentwood		"	"	"
Gilman, James			"	"	"
Gordon, Robert			"	"	"
Gordon, James			"	"	"
Gault, Adam	Londonderry	June 20	"	Sherburne's	"
Gault, Patrick	"		"	"	"
Griffith, John, Jr	Portsmouth	Feb. 13	Clerk	"	"
George, Joseph			Private	Prescott's	"
Gilman, Joshua			"	"	"
Gimpson, Thomas			"	"	"
4 Gove, Ebenezer	Hampton Falls		"	"	"
Gove, Joseph	" "		"	"	"
Green, Bradbury	" "	June 17	Lieut.	"	"
Gerrish, William	Dover	Feb. 13	Private	Hale's	"
Giles, John	"		Corp.	"	"
Glidden, William	"		Private	"	"
Gorman, James	"		"	"	"
Gowell, John	"		"	"	"
Grace, Nicholas	"		"	"	"
Gray, Reuben	"		Corp.	"	"
7 Gloster, John	Portsmouth	Feb. 13	Private	Mason's	"
8 Goudy, James		"	"	"	"
Gardner, David			"	Whidden's.	"
Greeley, Peter			"	"	"
Grove, John			"	"	"
Gale, Daniel			Officer		"

1 Promoted to Captain; no date.　2 Promoted Ensign July 9.　3 Promoted to Captain Oct. 1.　4 Died.　5 Captain of the Sloop Abigail.　6 Died Jan. 20, 1746.　7 Negro Slave of Theodore Atkinson.　8 Killed.

NEW HAMPSHIRE MEN IN THE LOUISBURG EXPEDITION, 1745.—*Cont.*

NAMES.	Residence.	Enlisted.	Rank.	Company.	Reg't.
Gilman, Ezekiel........	Exeter.........	Feb. 13	Major	....	Moore's.
1 Gilman, Robert........	"	"	Surgeon	....	"
Gilman, Jonathan......	Brentwood	April 15	Lieut.	....	"
Glidden, Charles......	....	....	Private	....	"
Godfrey, Jonathan	Hampton	Feb. 13	"	....	"
2 Hall, John............	....	....	"	Moore's....	"
2 Hall, Richard.........	....	....	"	"	"
Haley, Thomas........	....	....	"	"	"
Hodgdon, John........	....	....	"	"	"
Hodgdon, Israel.......	Newington	Feb. 13	"	"	"
Hunt, Abner..........	....	....	"	"	"
Huntress, Jonathan...	....	....	"	"	"
Huse, William........	....	....	"	"	"
Ham, Jotham	....	....	"	Fellows's..	"
Hooper, John.........	Portsmouth....	....	"	" "	"
Huntress, Christopher.	Newington	Feb. 13	Ensign	"	"
Hutchins, John	....	....	Private	"	"
3 Hale, Samuel	Portsmouth....	Feb. 13	Capt.	Hale's	"
Harris, Richard.......	"	"	Private	"	"
Hassam, Jacob........	Dover.........	"	"	"	"
Ham, Clement.........	"	"	Ensign	"	"
Hayes, Elisha.....	"	"	Private	"	"
Heard, Samuel..... ...	"	"	Sergt.	"	"
Hill, Ichabod	"	"	Private	"	"
Hoit, Charles	"	"	"	"	"
Hubbard, John H......	"	"	Drum'r	"	"
Hurell, Gideon........	Portsmouth....	"	Private	"	"
Huntress, Samuel......	Dover.........	"	"	"	"
Hussey, John.........	"	"	"	"	"
Harford, Nicholas.....	....	....	"	Wise's	"
Hall, John, Jr.........	....	....	"	....	"
4 Ham, Joseph..........	Portsmouth....	Feb. 13	"	....	"
4 Ham, Weymouth......	"	"	"	....	"
5 Ham, William	"	"	"	....	"
Hart, John	....	....	Lieut.	....	"
Hicks, John	Greenland....	Feb. 13	Private	....	"
5 Hilton, William.......	....	....	"	....	"
Hopkins, Edward......	Portsmouth....	....	"	....	"
Hutchins, George.....	"	Feb. 13	"	....	"
Ingalls, Peter.........	....	....	"	Williams's.	"
Jones, Thomas........	....	Feb. 13	"	Moore's....	"
Johnson, Thomas.....	....	....	"	Fellows's ..	"
Judkins, Joseph.......	....	....	"	Light's.....	"
1 Jackson, Joshua......	Portsmouth....	Feb. 13	"	....	"
Jackson, Elisha........	"	"	"	....	"
6 Jackson, Ebenezer	"	"	Sergt.	....	"
Johnson, Philip........	Greenland....	....	Private	....	"
Judkins, John........	....	....	"	....	"
Keniston, Joseph.....	....	Feb. 13	"	Moore's....	"
Knight, Richard......	....	....	"	Fellows's ..	"
Kelley, Daniel	....	....	"	Light's.....	"
Kennedy, Robert......	Londonderry..	June 20	Sergt.	Sherburne's	"
Kimball, Jonathan....	....	....	Psivate	Prescott's .	"
Keniston, William.....	....	Feb. 13	"	Hale's	"
Kenney, Richard	....	"	"	"	"
Kenney, Love.........	Dover.........	"	"	"	"
Kinkett, David........	....	....	"	"	"
Keniston, Samuel, Jr..	Greenland.....	Feb. 13	Mariner	Fernald's..	"
Kimming, Benjamin...	Exeter	"	Officer	Dudley's'..	"
Keniston, Benjamin...	....	....	Private	Whiddens..	"
7 Keniston, John........	....	Feb. 13	Mariner	Fernald's...	"
Keniston, Samuel, Jr..	....	"	"	"	"
King, George	Portsmouth....	....	Artificer	....	....

1 Wounded.   2 Some places, written Hull.   3 Promoted to Major, Oct. 17, 1745.
4 Taken prisoner.   5 Died.   6 Wounded, and died.   7 Killed.

NEW HAMPSHIRE MEN IN THE LOUISBURG EXPEDITION, 1745.—*Cont.*

Names.	Residence.	Enlisted.	Rank.	Company.	Reg't.
Leary, Jeremy.	....	Feb. 13	Private	Moore's....	Moore's.
[1] Loggin, John	....	"	"	"	"
Lamson, Nathaniel....	Exeter	....	"	Light's.....	"
Leary, Thomas........	....	....	"	"	"
Light, John	Exeter	June 17	Capt.	"	"
Lougee, Moses........	....	....	Private	"	"
Logan, Andrew.......	Londonderry..	June 20	"	Sherburne's	"
Locke, Thomas	....	....	"	Prescott's..	"
Lowell, James	Hampton Falls	....	"	"	"
Libby, Benjamin.......	Dover.........	Feb. 13	Sergt.	Hale's	"
Libby, Daniel.........	....	"	Private	"	"
Lowell, David........	....	....	"	Williams's.	"
Ladd, Daniel..........	Exeter	Feb. 13	Capt.	Ladd's......	"
[2] Ladd, Daniel, Jr.......	"	"	Private	"	"
Ladd, John...........	....	June 17	Capt.	"	"
Leavitt, Jonathan	.. ..	April 15	Private	Trefethen's	"
Leach, John..........	....	....	"	Wise's	"
[3] Ladd, Jonathan, Jr....	Kingston	Feb. 13	Surgeon	....	"
Langdon, Samuel......	Portsmouth....	Mar. 18	Chaplain	....	"
Lapish, William.......	....	....	Private	....	"
[3] Leavitt, Moses........	Hampton	Feb. 13	"	....	"
Leavitt, Joshua.......	....	....	"	....	"
Lewis, Benjamin.......	Portsmouth....	Feb. 13	"	....	"
Libby, John	....	....	"	....	"
Leavitt, Samuel.......	....	Feb. 13	"	....	"
[4] Lufkin, Isaac	....	"	Private	....	"
Moore, Samuel........	Portsmouth....	Feb. 12	Col.	Moore's....	"
Marston, William.....	....	Feb. 13	Private	"	"
Marston, James	....	"	"	"	"
Moulton, David.......	....	....	"	"	"
McMahone, Roger.....	....	....	"	Fellows's ..	"
Moore, Edward.......	....	....	Sergt.	"	"
Morgan, Andrew......	....	....	Private	"	"
Marcy, William.......	....	....	"	Light's.....	"
Marsh, James........	....	....	"	"	"
Moody, Clement......	Brentwood	....	"	"	"
[5] Marston, Jeremiah....	Hampton	Feb. 13	"	Sherburne's	"
McLaughlin, John.....	Londonderry..	June 20	"	"	"
McLenchan, James....	"	"	"	"	"
McNeil, John..........	Manchester....	"	"	"	"
McNeil, James........	"	"	"	"	"
Miller, Samuel........	Londonderry..	"	"	"	"
Miller, John..........	"	"	"	"	"
[3] Montgomery, Henry..	"	"	Ensign	"	"
[6] Montgomery Hugh....	Portsmouth....	Feb. 13	Private	"	"
Moulton, Henry.......	....	....	"	Prescott's..	"
Moulton, Thomas.....	....	....	"	"	"
[3] Moulton, Simon......	....	....	"	"	"
Merrow, Samuel.......	Rochester	....	"	Hale's......	"
Marston, John	Hampton	....	"	Williams's.	"
Mason, John T........	Portsmouth....	Feb. 13	Capt.	Mason's....	"
McGregor, Daniel.....	Londonderry..	June 20	"	McGregor's	"
Marston, Jonathan	....	....	Private	Whidden's.	"
Moulton, James	....	....	"	....	"
Marshall, Henry......	Brentwood	April 15	"	....	"
Marshall, Hawley.....	"	"	"	....	"
Martin, Michael.......	Portsmouth....	....	"	....	"
Martyn, Robert.......	"	....	"	....	"
Mason, Nathaniel.....	....	....	"	....	"
Mason, Benjamin.....	Hampton	....	"	....	"
Mason, Francis	Stratham......	....	"	....	"
[7] Mattoon, Richard.....	....	Feb. 13	Lieut.	....	"
Meader, Moses........	Durham.......	....	Private	....	"

[1] Promoted to Ensign, July 16, 1745. [2] Taken prisoner. [3] Died. [4] Wounded.
[5] Killed. [6] Killed. [7] Some places, Malloon.

NEW HAMPSHIRE MEN IN THE LOUISBURG EXPEDITION, 1745.—*Cont.*

NAMES.	Residence.	Enlisted.	Rank.	Company.	Reg't.
Merrill, Jacob..........	....	June 17	Ensign	....	Moore's.
Meserve, Nathaniel...	Portsmouth....	Feb. 13	Lt. Col.	Meserve's..	"
1 Meserve, Nathaniel,Jr.	"	"	Lieut.	"	"
Meserve, George	"	June 20	Capt.	"	"
2 Miller, Robert	Hampton Falls	Feb. 13	Private	....	"
Moody, John...........	....		"	....	"
Morgan, Abraham.....	Stratham	Feb. 13	"	....	"
3 Morgan, John..	Kingston	"	"	....	"
Moulton, Nathaniel....	Hampton		"	....	"
4 Newmarch, Thomas..	Portsmouth....	Feb. 13	Ensign	Fellows's..	"
Norton, Caleb.........	....	....	Private	Prescott's..	"
Nute, Paul.............	Dover.........	April 15	"	Trefethen's	"
Nelson, Joseph	Portsmouth....	Feb. 13	"	Hale's......	"
Nelson, John...........	"	"	"	....	"
5 Nelson, Leader........	"	"	"	....	"
Nelson, James.........	....	....	"	....	"
Peirce, Perham	....	Feb. 13	"	Moore's....	"
Perkins, George	....	"	"	"	"
Perry, John	....	"	"	"	"
Pinkham, John.........	....	....	"	Fellows's..	"
6 Pitman, Ezekiel, Jr....	Portsmouth....	Feb. 13	Ensign	"	"
Philbrick, Joseph......	....	....	Private	Light's.....	"
7 Prescott, William......	Epping	Feb. 13	"	"	"
Palmer, Growth........	....	"	"	Sherburne's	"
Page, David...........	Exeter	....	"	Prescott's..	"
8 Prescott, Jonathan....	....	June 17	Capt.	"	"
Prescott, Joseph.......	....	....	Private	"	"
3 Prescott, John...... ..	Kingston	....	"	"	"
Pressey, Paul..........	"	....	"	....	"
Perkins, Thomas.......	Rochester	Feb. 13	Corp.	Hale's......	"
Perkins, Nathaniel	....	"	Private	"	"
Paine, John	Newcastle	....	"	Whidden's.	"
Peavey, Joseph........	....	....	"	"	"
Partridge. Jonathan...	Portsmouth...	Feb. 13	"	....	"
Pease, Samuel..........	Newmarket....	....	"	....	"
Pendexter, Edward, Jr.	....	....	"	....	"
Perkins, Robert	....	Feb. 13	Ensign	....	"
Philbrick, Josiah......	....	Oct. 10	"	....	"
3 Philbrick, Simon.....	....	....	Private	....	"
Pickering, Thomas	....	Feb. 13	Ensign	....	"
Pierce, Joseph.........	Portsmouth....	Mar. 16	Sur. ch'f	....	"
Pinkham, Solomon	Dover..........	Feb. 13	Armorer	....	"
Quimby, Eliphalet.....	....	....	Private	Light's.....	"
Rand, William........	Newcastle.....	Feb. 13	"	Moore's....	"
Randall, William	....	....	"	Fellows's ..	"
Rawlings, Stephen	....	....	"	"	"
Rawlings, Samuel......	Newington	....	"	"	"
Read, Solomon........	Dover..........	....	"	"	"
Roberts, Isaac.........	....	....	"	"	"
Rundlett, Satchel.....	....	Feb. 13	"	Sherburne's	"
Robinson, Benjamin...	....	....	"	Light's.....	"
Rowe, Daniel	....	....	"	Prescott's..	"
Rowe, Nathan.........	Hampton Falls	....	"	"	"
Rowe, Robert	....	....	"	"	"
Richardson, Samuel...	....	....	"	Hale's	"
Ring, Eliphalet	Portsmouth....	Feb. 13	"	"	"
Roberts, Samuel.	Dover.........	"	"	"	"
Roberts, Thomas	"	"	"	"	"
Rowell, Enoch.........	Chester	"	"	Williams's.	"
Rand, William, Jr.....	....	....	"	....	"
9 Rawlings, Joseph......	Exeter.........	....	"	....	"
Read, Samuel..........	....	....	"	....	"
Redman, Joseph.......	Hampton	....	"	....	"

1 Taken prisoner. Aug. 1, promoted to Lieutenant.   2 Arm shot off.   3 Died.
4 Promoted to Lieutenant, Oct. 5, 1745.   5 Taken prisoner.   6 Promoted to
Lieutenant, June 20, 1745.   7 Lost a leg.   8 Died April 12, 1746.   9 Wounded,
June 7.

NEW HAMPSHIRE MEN IN THE LOUISBURG EXPEDITION, 1745.—*Cont.*

Names.	Residence.	Enlisted.	Rank.	Company.	Reg't.
Robie, Samuel	Chester	Feb. 13	Lieut.	....	Moore's.
Robinson, Charles.....	....	....	Private	....	"
1 Sanborn, Abner.......	....	Feb. 13	"	Moore's....	"
Spriggs, William	....	"	"	"	"
Studley, William.......	....	"	"	"	"
Senter, Abraham.......	....	....	"	Fellows's..	"
Sherburne, Edward ...	....	....	"	"	"
Stevens, John.........	Newington	....	"	"	"
Sanborn, Josiah.......	....	....	"	Lights'	"
Savage, Moses........	....	....	"	"	"
Scribner, Samuel	....	....	"	"	"
Severans, John	....	....	"	"	"
Sinkler, Ebenezer.....	Exeter	....	"	"	"
Sinkler, Samuel.......	....	....	"	"	"
Stockbridge, Abram...	Stratham	....	"	"	"
Sherburne, Henry.....	Portsmouth ...	Feb. 13	Captain	Sherburne's	"
Sherburne, Joseph.....	"	June 6	"	"	"
Sherburne, Edward....	"	....	Private	"	"
Sims, Samuel..... ...	....	....	"	"	"
Stockbridge, Warren..	....	....	"	"	"
Stevens, Ephraim......	....	....	"	Prescott's..	"
Swain, William........	Hampton Falls	....	"	"	"
Sweet, Robert.........	....	....	"	"	"
Salter, Richard........	Dover.........	....	"	Hale's	"
2 Sam..................	Portsmouth....	....	"	"	"
Sanborn, Marston.....	....	....	"	"	"
Smith, Archibald	Dover.........	....	"	"	"
Smith, John	....	....	"	"	"
Stanton, Benjamin. ...	Dover	Feb. 13	"	"	"
Stanton, Benjamin, Jr.	Somersworth..	"	"	"	"
Stoodley, Jonathan....	Portsmouth ...	....	"	"	"
Samborn, John..... ...	....	....	"	Williams's.	"
Samborn, Ebenezer....	....	....	"	"	"
Shaw, Benjamin.......	Hampton Falls	....	"	"	"
Seaward, William.....	So. Hampton..	Feb. 13	Captain	Seaward's .	"
Smith, James.........	....	....	Private	Wise's	"
Sleeper, Joseph.......	Kingston	Feb. 13	Ensign	Ladd's	"
Sanborn, Shubael......	Hampton	....	Private	....	"
Sargent, Nathaniel Jr.	"	Mar. 20	Surgeon	....	"
Shaw, Josiah..........	"	Feb. 13	Private	....	"
Sheafe, Jacob.........	Portsmouth....	Oct. 5	Comsy.	....	"
Sleeper, Moses........	Kingston	June 17	Lieut.	....	"
Sleeper, Henry	Portsmouth....	Feb. 13	Private	....	"
Sleeper, John	Hampton	....	"	....	"
Studley, John	....	....	"	....	"
Thompson, Alexander.	....	Feb. 13	"	Moore's....	"
Tobey, Samuel........	....	"	"	"	"
Towle, Jabez..........	....	"	"	"	"
Treadwell, William E..	Portsmouth....	"	Comsy.	"	"
Turner, John..........	"	"	Private	"	"
Thompson, Samuel	....	....	"	Fellows's..	"
1 Thomas, John.........	... .	Feb. 13	"	Sherburne's	"
Thompson, James	....	"	Corpl.	"	"
Thompson, William ...	Rochester	"	Private	Hale's	"
Titcomb, John	Dover.........	"	"	"	"
Tibbetts, Samuel......	"	"	Corpl.	"	"
Tilton, Benjamin......	Hampton Falls	.. ..	Private	Prescott's..	"
Taylor, James.........	....	....	"	Williams's.	"
Tilton, Jacob..........	Newmarket ...	Mar. 1	Captain	Tilton's	"
Trefethen, Abraham...	Newcastle....-.	Apr. 15	"	Trefethen's	"
3 Tucker, Lewis	" ....-	Feb. 13	Mariner	Fernald's..	"
Thing, Peter	Brentwood	....	Officer	....	"
4 Thomas, Benjamin ...	Portsmouth ...	Feb. 13	Private	....	"
Thompson, George....	"	....	"	....	"

1 Died.   2 An Indian.   3 Taken prisoner, died.   4 Wounded.

NEW HAMPSHIRE MEN IN THE LOUISBURG EXPEDITION, 1745.—*Cont.*

Names.	Residence.	Enlisted.	Rank.	Company.	Reg't.
[1] Thornton, Mathew.....	Londonderry..	Mar. 1	Surgeon	....	....
Tilton, Daniel..........	....	....	Private	....	Moore's.
[2] Trefethen, Henry Jr...	Newcastle	Feb. 13	"	....	"
Trydick, Henry.........	....	....	"	....	"
[2] Tufts, Thomas..........	....	Feb. 13	Ensign	....	"
[3] Veasey, Jeremiah......	... .	June 17	"	Light's.....	"
Vittem, William	Hampton	Feb. 13	Private	Moore's.....	"
[4] Vaughan, William.....	Portsmouth ...	"	Lt. Col.	....	....
Vittem, William, Jr....	Hampton	....	Private	....	Moore's.
White, Nathaniel R....	Stratham	Feb. 13	Sergt.	Moore's....	"
Wilson, John....	....	"	Private	"	"
Wallace, Archibald....	....	....	"	Fellows's ..	"
Weare, Moses..........	....	....	"	"	"
Welch, John..	....	....	"	"	"
Wherrin, James	....	....	"	"	"
Wherrin, Isaac	....	....	"	"	"
Woodham, John.......	....	....	"	"	"
Waldron, Richard K...	Dover..........	Feb. 13	"	Hale's	"
Watson, Samuel	"	"	"	"	"
Wingate, Moses.......	"	"	Lieut.	"	"
Wingate, Daniel	"	"	Private	"	"
Ward, James..........	....	....	"	Light's.....	"
Watson, Thomas......	....	....	"	"	"
Wells, John	....	....	"	"	"
Winslow, Joshua	.. ..	Sept. 30	Lieut.	"	"
Welch, David	....	....	Private	Sherburne's	"
Wright, Ebenezer	....	Apr. 15	Ensign	"	"
Ward, Daniel	....	. ...	Private	Prescott's .	"
[5] Weare, Joseph........	Kensington...	....	"	"	"
Weed, Joseph....	....	....	"	"	"
[6] Worthen, Ezekiel......	Kensington ...	June 17	Ensign	"	"
Weare, Nathaniel......	Hampton Falls	....	Private	William's..	"
[2] Williams, Edward.....	"	Mar. 2	Captain	"	"
Waldron, Thomas W..	Dover..........	Feb. 13	"	Waldron's .	"
Watson, Jonathan.....	Hampton Falls	....	Private	Ladd's......	"
Whidden, James......	....	Feb. 13	Captain	Whidden's.	"
Wise. John............	....	Apr. 15	"	Wise's	"
Wood, James	....	Mar. 18	Sur.Mate	....	"
Wadleigh, Theophilus.	Epping	....	Private	....	"
Walden. John.........	....	....	"	....	"
Warren, Walter........	Portsmouth ...	....	"	....	"
Waters, Samuel.......	"	....	"	....	"
[7] Weymouth, Shadrick..	"	Feb. 13	"	....	"
Wheelwright, Jeremiah	....	"	Lieut.	... .	"
Whidden, Michael.....	Portsmouth ...	"	Private	....	"
Whidden, Nicholas....	....	"	Sergt.	....	"
White, Samuel.........	....	"	Lieut.	....	"
Whitton, Samuel......	....	....	Captain	....	"
Wormall, Daniel	Brentwood	Feb. 13	Ensign	....	"
Young, Eleazer	Dover..........	"	Sergt.	Hale's.....	"
Young, Joseph........	....	....	Private	Sherburne's	"
Yeatton, Philip	Somersworth..	Apr. 15	Ensign	....	"
York, Richard	Exeter..........	Feb. 13	Private	....	"
Young, Hezekiah......	Kingston	....	"	....	"

[1] Richmonds, Mass. Reg't. [2] Died. [3] Promoted to lieutenant Oct. 1, 1745. [4] Commissioned by Mass. [5] Promoted ensign Aug. 11, 1745. [6] Promoted to lieutenant Oct. 1, 1745. [7] Taken prisoner.

NEW HAMPSHIRE MEN IN THE LOUISBURG EXPEDITION, 1745.—*Cont.*

Names.	Residence.	Enlisted.	Rank	Company.	Reg't.
Atherton, Philip			Private		
Bishop, Baly			Sergt.		
Blaucher, Edward			Private		
Braman, Thomas			Drum'r		
Campbell, Jeremiah			Private		
Caperon, John			"		
Cobb, Richard			Sergt.		
Crossman, Henry			Private		
Day, Edward			"		
Dorman, Micajah			"		
Esty, Benjamin			Sergt.		
Fillebrown, Thomas			Private		
Fisher, Nehemiah			Sergt.		
Fisher, Abijah			Private		
Fisher, John			"		
Fisher, Eleazer			"		
Forrest, John			"		
Forrest, Samuel			"		
French, Ephraim			"		
French, Jacob			"		
Glen, Richard			Corpl.		
Grover, Thomas			Private		
Hodges, Eliphalet			Corpl.		
Hodges, Benjamin			Private		
Hounestman, Heber			"		
Lane, Zepheniah			"		
Lyon, Elkanon			Clerk		
Napp, Aaron			Private		
Rogers, John			"		
Sheldon, Ephraim			"		
Thayer, Ephraim			"		
Thayer, Philip			"		
Tiffany, Joseph			Corpl.		
Tiffany, Robert			"		
Turner, Ebenezer			Private		
Weeks, John			"		
White, Abraham			"		
White, Daniel			"		
Wood, Benjamin			"		

[*Shirley to Wentworth.*]

Boston, March 4, 1745.

Sir, As it will be uncertain where Mr Vaughan will be upon the arrival of this I am obliged to trouble you with 100^{lh} N. Tenour (by the bearer) to pay to those men, wch he shall have enlisted over & above the 150 to be aggregated to your Regiment, and to desire him to see y^t the men are march'd to Boston instantly to fill up the Incomplete Companies belonging te Colonel Hale's Regiment, wch will be there by the time those men get to Boston, or if he marches 'em to Charleston it will do: I must refer you for everything else at present to Mr Bastide, who will dine wth you on Monday—I am sorry I am obliged to trouble you wth the Letter wch accompanies this, at this improper time; But I could not avoid, from the Importunity of the Council, and expectation of the assembly, doing it longer—I will write you further upon it by next post and must now subscribe my self in much haste and Truth

Your Exc^{ys} most obedient Humble servant

W. Shirley

His Exc^y Govr Wentworth

[The men referred to in the foregoing were raised in New Hampshire, over and above its own quota, to help Massachusetts fill its quota for the Louisburg expedition. See Vol. V, 943.—Editor N. H. State Papers.]

From the above letter of Governor Shirley of Massachusetts it would appear that the thirty-nine men in the foregoing roll were from New Hampshire, but as it is uncertain, have put them in a separate roll.

THE CELEBRATION.

The *American Historical Register* has granted the writer permission to copy from its report of the proceedings at the celebration, in the July number for 1895, which he has done, in an abridged form.

THE LOUISBURG MONUMENT.

ERECTED BY THE SOCIETY OF COLONIAL WARS. UNVEILED JUNE 17, 1895.

The handsome marble column erected by the Society of Colonial Wars at Louisburg, Cape Breton, to commemorate the one hundred and fiftieth anniversary of the siege and surrender of the fortress of Louisburg to the New England troops under General Pepperell, was unveiled June 17. It was a successful event in every way. The weather was propitious to outdoor services and thousands of people from the surrounding country and from Halifax and Sydney, witnessed the function. Every State Society of Colonial Wars was represented, many members of the New York and New England Chapters were present on their private yachts with parties of friends.

The British war ship *Canada* was present and gaily decorated with bunting, as were the vessels in port and many private residences.

4

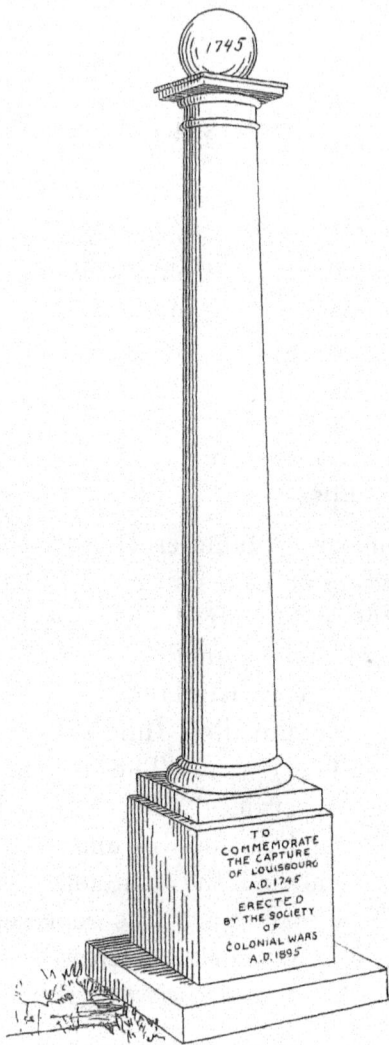

1745

TO
COMMEMORATE
THE CAPTURE
OF LOUISBOURG
A.D. 1745

ERECTED
BY THE SOCIETY
OF
COLONIAL WARS
A.D. 1895

THE LOUISBURG MONUMENT.

The French Canadians entered heartily into
the jollification, although the monument was to
commemorate a victory over their ancestors   Fre-
quent mention was made by the speakers of the
valor and chivalry of the French, and the hope was
expressed that the French republic would always
be on friendly relations with the United States and
Great Britain.   The land on which the monument
is erected was donated by a Frenchman.

The assemblage was called to order at noon, in
the King's Bastion of the ruins of the fortress, by
the chairman of the Society's Monument Committee, Mr. Howland Pell, of New York, with some
appropriate remarks.   After prayer by the Rev. Dr.
Salter, of Burlington, Iowa, the following address
of Mr. Frederick J. de Peyster, of New York, governor-general of the Society, was read by Mr. Pell:

*Mr. Governor, Gentlemen of the Society of Colonial Wars,
and Guests:*   We have assembled here to-day among these
storied ruins to dedicate the first—the very first—monument
ever erected by the people of the Great Republic to commemorate the greatest triumph achieved by their colonial
ancestors.

It is the greatest triumph, because it is the only instance
recorded in history of the victory of a body of irregulars,
led by a civilian, over well-trained and gallant foes.   It was
the success of shopkeepers, artisans, fishermen, farmers, and
clerks commanded by a mere merchant, planned by a law-
yer utterly ignorant of the art of war, over the regular
soldiers of the first military power of Europe, led by well-
trained, experienced, and gallant commanders, and intrenched within the strongest fortress of the New World.

The enterprise was a mad one, but it succeeded.   Victory
without the English fleet would have been impossible.   The

English fleet was at first refused, but it arrived in good time to complete the victory. Thirty years ago, Goldwin Smith said :

" The English yeomanry are no longer to be found in England, the descendants of the brave youths who followed the standards of Cromwell and Ireton no longer breathe British air ; but they are not extinct ; to-day you may find them beneath the standards of Grant and of Sherman."

What renders this triumph of the Anglo-Saxon race the more glorious is that it was won over worthy foes. The fortress which capitulated 150 years ago to-day was held by the first soldiers of Europe, the warriors of the "Grand Monarque." Few laurels can be won by defeating a horde of Asiatic slaves, but to tear the Lilies from the citadel was, indeed, a splendid achievement.

The laurels won here were won from no poltroons, but from the brave, romantic, chivalrous, but unfortunate children of glorious France. The glory of this day is enough for all. Enough for English and American on the one hand and the gallant soldiers of Louis on the other. Both sides were equally brave, but fortune, as usual, favored the bigger battalions. Captain Mahan is right. The true secret of England's empire, of her long roll of victories, is her sea power. Had France instead of England controlled the sea, French would be to-day the language of Boston, Philadelphia, and New York. It was this long century of struggle which decided the fate of the continent, and hence the gratitude which we feel to those who battled so long, so gallantly, and so successfully for the Cross of St. George.

Our Society of Colonial Wars is devoted to doing justice to this very period, to the men who raised the scattered and attenuated fringe of settlements along the Atlantic into the mighty republic which is to-day the peer of the greatest power on earth. We wish that the unconquerable energy, the heroic courage, the devoted patriotism of those earlier days when Americans really became Americans, should remain the distinguishing characteristics of our race to the end of time.

And therefore we erect this monument to the memory of our heroic ancestors and as an inspiration to heroism for all generations of Americans.

Mr. Everett Pepperell Wheeler, of New York, one of the few living descendants of the hero of Louisburg, General Pepperell, and a member of the New York State Society of Colonial Wars, delivered the following oration of the day:

Mr. Governor, Gentlemen of the Society of Colonial Wars, and Guests: Heaven smiles on our undertaking. The northwest wind has driven away the clouds and fogs of the past week. Under the blue Cape Breton sky we commemorate achievements that, in their ultimate result, gave to the two great North American commonwealths their goodly heritage.

The Roman historian tells us that the leaders of his time used to say that when they looked on the statues of their ancestors their souls were stirred with a passion of virtue. It was not the marble, nor the features that in themselves had force. But the memory of their noble deeds kindled a flame in the breasts of their descendants which could not be quenched until their actions had equaled the renown and worth of their fathers.

In like manner we dedicate this monument in a spirit of gratitude to God and noble emulation for the heroism of man. No narrow spirit of local self-gratulation has brought us hither. We are glad to recognize that British sailors and colonial soldiers shared in the difficulties and dangers of the siege whose successful issue we celebrate to-day. And we are swift to acknowledge the courage and endurance of the garrison, who, cut off from succor and short of provi-

sious, offered brave resistance for seven weeks to the British
fleet and the regiments of Massachusetts, New Hampshire,
and Connecticut.

In the Parliament of Quebec questions have been put to
the government, indicating that the member who asked
them thought that this monument was erected in the spirit
of triumph over a fallen foe. To him I reply that we
have not thus learned the lessons of history. This column points upward to the stars, and away from the petty
jealousies that man the earth. It will tell, we trust, to many
generations, the story of the courage, heroic fortitude, and
manly energy of those who fought behind the ramparts, as
well as of those who fought in the trenches. Some histo-
rians, it is true, have underrated the bravery of the defenders
of the city, and even asserted that they surrendered before
a breach was made in their walls, and when they might well
have held out for months. The best answer to this is contained in an original document which gives the most
authentic account of the siege : Governor Shirley's letter to
the Duke of Newcastle. This was certified by Pepperell
himself and by Waldo, Moore, Lothrop, and Gridley. It
gives the following graphic description of the condition of
the fortress when Du Chambon surrendered :

"And now, the Grand Battery being in our possession,
the Island Battery (esteemed by the French the Palladium
of Louisburg) so much annoyed from the Lighthouse Battery, that they could not entertain the hope of keeping it
much longer ; the enemy's northeast battery being damaged, and so much exposed to the fire from our advanced
battery, that they could not stand to their guns ; the circu-
lar battery ruined, and all its guns but three dismounted,
whereby the Harbour was disarmed of all its principal batteries ; the west gate of the city being demolished, and a
breach made in the adjoining wall ; the west flank of the
King's Bastion almost ruined ; and most of the other guns,
which had been mounted during the time of the siege being

silenced; all the houses and other buildings within the city
(some of which were quite demolished) so damaged, that
but one among them was left unhurt; the enemy extremely
harassed by their long confinement within their casemates,
and other covered holes, and their stock of ammunition
being almost exhausted, Mr. Du Chambon sent out a flag
of truce."

The men who stood in the trenches at Louisburg or
dragged their cannon across its morasses were the best
men of their colonies. They came hither inspired by no
greed for conquest. Their expedition was really a defen-
sive one. Their commerce had been assailed, their fron-
tier settlements ravaged by hostile Indians, their wives
and children massacred or carried into captivity. Louisburg was the harbor where the French privateers found
refuge, and whence marauding expeditions sallied forth.
Its massive walls were twenty-five years in building.
Time has dealt hardly with these, but their ruins still bear
witness to what was called at the time, the Dunkirk of
America. The harbor which they covered you behold
before you, landlocked and secure from the storms of this
rockbound coast. The Island Battery and the Grand Battery barred all hostile entrance. And the city had mag-
azines from which all Canada might be supplied.

The immediate occasion of the Louisburg expedition
was an appeal for aid from Nova Scotia. In the archives
of that province you will find a letter from Governor Mas-
carene to Governor Shirley, of Massachusetts. It was
written at Annapolis Royall, December, 1744. In this
your governor tells the story of the outbreak of war.

The honor of suggesting the Louisburg expedition has
been claimed by several. Probably the thought occurred
to more than one. The New England people were ripe
for the attempt. Their state of mind at the time is well
described by Belknap, the historian of New Hampshire:

" There are certain latent sparks in human nature which, by a collision of causes, are sometimes brought to light, and, when once excited, their operations are not easily controlled. In undertaking anything hazardous, there is a necessity for extraordinary vigor of mind and a degree of confidence and fortitude which shall raise us above the dread of danger and dispose us to run a risk which the cold maxims of prudence would forbid. The people of New England have at various times shown such an enthusiastic ardor, which has been excited by the example of their ancestors and their own exposed situation. It was never more apparent, and perhaps never more necessary, than on occasion of this expedition. Nor ought it to be forgotten that several circumstances, which did not depend on human foresight, greatly favored this undertaking."

The General Court of Massachusetts decided, on January 29, by a majority of one vote, to undertake the expedition. Immediately preparations were made with the utmost speed. Those who had opposed the plan, because of its danger, vied with its supporters in activity to promote its success.

It is not surprising that the enterprise should have aroused the enthusiasm of men like the colonists of that day. They were the most resolute and fearless of a resolute and fearless race. Religious zeal had led some to this country. Love of adventure had influenced others. They were inured to hardship by constant struggle with nature. They had built their own houses and their own ships, had cleared forests and ploughed fields.

The exigency of their situation had made them ready for any emergency. There were few factories in America, and the necessaries of life were largely supplied by the industry of the hamlets. The embroidered waistcoats and purple coats of the gentry, as you see them in the portraits of Copley and Smybert, came from home, as England still was called. But the garments of the sailors and farmers, who battered down the walls of Louisburg, were woven around their firesides in the long winter evenings.

And then we must remember that the people of the thirteen colonies were a commercial and seafaring people. They dwelt in a narrow strip of land extending along the Atlantic coast.

Thus have I tried to sketch the characteristics of the Americans of 1745. In times of peril such characteristics always find embodiment in a leader. It is common and easy to say that great men are but the expression of their time and lead it only in the sense that the spray leads the billow. That is but half the truth. When God gives to mankind the inestimable gift of a great man, he does, it is true, represent the spirit of his age. But he leads it, as the moon does the tides. Happy the people who appreciate such a man and are filled by his spirit, as the Bay of Fundy in every creek and inlet is filled by the advancing flood. It was fortunate for the colonies that in the emergency of 1745 there was a leader whom they trusted, and who was wise enough to discard the visionary schemes of others; brave enough to face the veterans of France, intrenched behind the walls which the skill and experience of Vauban had planned, and self-sacrificing enough to leave home and business, and all that made life pleasant and sweet, to endure the hardship and peril of this expedition, which Parkman calls "a mad scheme"— but which Pepperell and his followers dared to undertake.

I could not do justice to the occasion or the subject if I failed to speak for a moment of his remarkable career. He was a notable instance of the versatility and adaptiveness which the life of those days compelled. He was a successful merchant. He was a gallant soldier, accustomed from early youth to draw the sword in defense of his home and country. He had been in actual service against the In-

dians before he was twenty-one. It might have been said
of him, as it was of Wolfe, that he,

> Where'er he fought,
> Put so much of his heart into his act,
> That his example had a magnet's force,
> And all were swift to follow, whom all loved.

He was for twenty-nine years chief justice of the Court
of Common Pleas for Maine. He was an active and con-
spicuous member of His Majesty's Council for the colony
of Massachusetts. It is but just to him to add that his
religion was not disfigured by bigotry or intolerance. It
was an evident power in his life, but it always respected
the religion of others.

And now let me return to the story of the expedition
itself. I will not dwell upon its details. Representatives
of societies from various states have spoken of what each
colony did to promote its success. Massachusetts (which
then included Maine) certainly did the most. She was
the richest and most populous. But New Hampshire and
Connecticut did much, and New York, New Jersey, Rhode
Island, and Pennsylvania came forward to aid, though no
troops of theirs were in the trenches. A Rhode Island
sloop of war rendered essential service.

When we remember how difficult communication between the colonies was at the time of which we are speak-
ing, we shall wonder that they acted so much in concert—
not that they did no more. The mails were infrequent—
roads were poor. Oftentimes the travelers in a stage
coach were obliged to get out and lift the wheels out of
the mud in which they sunk to the hubs. No one had
even dreamed of railroad or electric telegraph. The won-
derful power of steam was unknown. It will help us to
realize the obstacles which beset any concerted action on
the part of the colonies when we remember that even in
the old mother country roads were so bad, and the trans-
mission of intelligence so slow, that the Chevalier had

been in Scotland nearly three weeks before the news reached Edinburgh. The tidings of the surrender of Louisburg did not reach Boston until July 3, sixteen days after the event, and were first known in New York a week later.

Such were the difficulties that our fathers had to face. Yet, withal, they had encouragement. Providence had favored their cause. The harvest of 1744 had been abundant, the winter was mild, the frontiers of New England had been unmolested, unexpected supplies arrived from Great Britain. The Grand Battery was not well fortified on the land side. The city had deprived itself of provisions to furnish the East India fleet and squadron for its recent voyage to France, and the *Vigilante*, which brought supplies, was captured by Warren. The weather during the siege was generally fine. The colonial troops captured in the Grand Battery, and fished up at the careening basin, the heavy cannon which they needed.

But all these would have availed nothing had it not been for the courage, the perseverance, the aptitude of the men who took advantage of these favoring circumstances, and brought their fleet of 100 vessels, with the little army of 4,050 men, safely to Canseau. There, to their great delight, on April 23, appeared Warren's squadron. Thence they sailed to Louisburg; on April 30, the troops landed, and after seven weeks of toil and peril, diversified, as we learn, when the soldiers were off duty, by games and sports, the fortress was theirs.

Their hardihood and daring are described in the words of one of the gallant French garrison as repeated by Gibson in the journal before-mentioned :

" This gentleman, I say, told me that he had not had his clothes off his back, either by night or day, from the first commencement of the siege. He added, moreover, that in all the histories he had ever read, he never met with an instance of so bold and presumptuous an attempt; that 'twas almost impracticable, as any one could think, for only three or four thousand raw, undisciplined men to lay siege to such a strong, well-fortified city, such garrisons, batteries, etc. For should any one have asked me, said he, what number of men would have been sufficient to have carried on that very enterprise, he should have answered not less than thirty thousand. To this he subjoined that he never heard of or ever saw such courage and intrepidity in such a handful of men, who regarded neither shot nor bombs. But what was still more surprising than all the rest, he said, was this, namely, to see batteries raised in a night's time, and more particularly the Fascine battery, which was not five-and-twenty rods from the city wall; and to see guns that were forty-two pounders dragged by the English from their grand battery, notwithstanding it was two miles distant, at least, and the road, too, very rough."

The tidings of the surrender were received throughout the colonies with the utmost enthusiasm. The contemporary accounts are too graphic not to be quoted:

"Now the churl and the niggard became generous, and even the poor forgot their poverty, and in the evening the whole town (Boston) appeared, as it were, in a blaze, almost every house being finely illuminated."

And now, let us pause for a moment and ask what was the result of this expedition. Do its consequences merit a monument? At first sight, apparently not. The capture of Louisburg is one of those historical events which was fruitful of great results, but which, for the most part, are slow in germination. Immediately it secured the cod fishery to the colonists for three years; it cut the French fishermen off from the Banks for a like period; it destroyed the French Atlantic trade for 1745; it gave the English a prize which enabled them to buy back Madras at the treaty of Aix la Chapelle. India was more valuable in the eyes of the Duke of Newcastle than all the Atlantic colonies.

But the remote consequences of this expedition far transcend in importance these immediate ones. It was a school of arms for the colonial troops. Gridley, who planned the parallels and trenches at Louisburg, laid out also the fortifications of Bunker Hill.

Its success showed the colonies their power and the necessity for their union. It showed them, too, that in the councils of Great Britain their affairs were of minor importance. This was a dreadful shock to the loyal love of the old home which then was general in the colonies. On the other hand, the capture of Louisburg pointed out to William Pitt the possibility of the conquest of the whole of Canada, and paved the way for that.

In the next war Canada was conquered, and the English colonists freed from the fear of attack from their neighbor on the north. The expenses of this war and the consequent demands of the British exchequer, led the ministry to tax the colonies. America resisted, and the result was the American Revolution. By an extraordinary turn in the wheel of time, the French assisted the old English colonies to become an independent nation, while the old French colonies remained the property of Great Britain.

It is now one hundred and fifty years since the surrender of Louisburg. It is one hundred and twelve years since the treaty of Paris recognized the independence of the United States and confirmed to Great Britain the possession of Canada. Surely the rancor of the old wars ought by this time to be burned completely out. Surely we can now agree that the development of these countries during all that time has been promoted by the result of those old wars. And despite, perhaps partly in consequence of, the magnitude and costliness of the fleets and armies of to-day, we may believe that the ties of Christian faith, the links of mutual trade, the bands of friendship, the swift steamer, and the swifter electric current have bound us so closely together that English and French and American armies shall never more meet on the battlefield. We vie in the peaceful contests of art and science, and will settle the inevitable disputes by arbitration. There are social problems before us, as difficult of solution as any that have vexed the past. The very complication of the interlacing nerves of our modern civilization, which offers so many obstacles to war and binds nations over to keep the peace, is producing disorders and dangers within each state that require nicer surgery than that of the sword or the bayonet.

It is then with faces to the future that we dedicate this monument to the memory of all the brave men who fought and fell at Louisburg, whether under the Cross of St. George or the Lilies of France. The morning sun will illumine its summit. The sunset ray will gild its massive and simple outline. The storms and fogs of Cape Breton will gather round it. In sunshine and storm alike, let it tell to all mankind that peace has her victories, no less renowned than war; that the courage and resolution of the fathers live in the hearts of their children; that we are prepared to face the conflicts, the difficulties and the perils of the coming century in firm reliance upon the protecting care of the same God who was with our fathers and will be with all who are loyal to Him to the end of time.

Addresses were also made by Dr. Mackay of the N. S. Historical Society, D. H. Ingraham, United States consul-general for Nova Scotia, and representatives of the various State Societies of Colonial Wars, when the monument was unveiled by His Honor Lieutenant-Governor Daly of Nova Scotia, on behalf of His Excellency the Earl of Aberdeen, governor-general of Canada; and salutes were fired.

After benediction by the Rev. T. Fraser Draper, rector of St. Bartholomew's Church, Louisburg, the members of the Society of Colonial Wars and their guests dined together.

In the evening, at the Sydney hotel, the mayor and recorder of Sydney and warden of the municipality presented an address of welcome, congratulation, and thanks to the visiting members of the Society of Colonial Wars. Happy responses were made by several of the visitors and by A. G. Jones, and a very pleasant time was brought to a close by singing "Auld Lang Syne."

www.ingramcontent.com/pod-product-compliance
Lightning Source LLC
Chambersburg PA
CBHW052217090426
42741CB00010B/2579